Torchsong for Grace

Torchsong for Grace

Theodore Michael Christou

First Edition

Wet Ink Books
www.WetInkBooks.com
WetInkBooks@gmail.com

Torchsong for Grace
by Theodore Michael Christou

Cover Image – Theodore Michael Christou
Inside Images – Theodore Michael Christou
Cover Design – Richard M. Grove
Layout and Design – Richard M. Grove

Typeset in Garamond
Printed and bound in Canada
Distributed in USA by Ingram,
    – to set up an account – 1-800-937-0152

Library and Archives Canada Cataloguing in Publication

Title: Torchsong for Grace / Theodore Michael Christou.
Names: Christou, Theodore Michael, author
Description: First edition.
Identifiers: Canadiana 20250314630 | ISBN 9781998324286 (softcover)
Subjects: LCGFT: Poetry.
Classification: LCC PS8605.H7554 T67 2025 | DDC C811/.6—dc23

Introduction

this book is a torchsong. it is a day of prayer, a walk through the hours, a cycle shaped by monks for centuries.

here, time is measured by the body's turning toward god. it is marked by the way the light breaks and recedes, by the stillness that settles at midnight, by the pulse of the earth itself, the quiet thrum of a world held in its own deep purpose.

the poems are arranged as these hours, a movement from dawn to dark where prayer rises and returns.

orthros *offers the awakening of light, a sudden brightness that breaks the night with grace.* ***the first hour*** *gathers the day's labor, the careful work of folding, mending, and lifting that belongs to prayer.* ***the third hour*** *opens with fire and inspiration, the first flame of the holy spirit.* ***the sixth hour*** *holds the height of trial and sorrow, the weight of a world at its noonday.* ***the ninth hour*** *carries grief into mercy, the exhale of a world that has suffered and found release. vespers is a gathering of thanks as evening settles, a quiet moment of gratitude before the final darkness.* ***midnight*** *closes in silence and prepares the ground for what lies beyond the day, a stillness that precedes a new beginning.*

these are the hours of a single voice. it carries many faces: the monk at prayer, the scholar with a page, the poet in the street. each one a fragment of a larger truth. these figures are joined in a single life, one held in both fragility and radiance.

the language is direct, a steady speech that mirrors the clarity of water after rain. each word enters on equal ground, unadorned, stripped of its formalities, carrying sense and sound by its own force. it is a language that seeks to be a form of prayer in itself, a breath held and released in each line, in each word.

for grace, everlasting

orthros

orthros opens in the first wash of light.

the hour gathers the world into sight and breath.

the poems incline toward awakening, with river, tree, and sky as companions of beginning

they invite the reader to receive the morning as clarity, as gift, and as task.

in the breath of the tree

the forest exhales through bark.
the tall tree creaks,
its limbs drawn long
in the daytime's slow pull.
strain gathers in my body
bone stretched,
each step drawn, a pulse of pain.

the tree moves as i move,
rooted, living.
its trunk leans,
then lifts with the gust
like sap drawn up in wind.

squirrels pause in the branches,
still beneath the shimmer of spray.
their bodies quiet,
fur touched by mist.
the geese rest among the banks,
wings folded
like linen pressed across the chest.

the ground opens, longing.
rain seeps into soil,
softening the path.
my feet sink gently,
heel to toe,
each step a slow conversation
with the muck.

pain steps beside me,
a shadow keeping time.
it rises and falls
like wind through the trees,
circling, returning,
always present.

then comes the quiet.
air dim with rain and hush.
i stop.
the tree eases its lean.
a thread of rain slides down my spine.
we breathe,
as one held shape in the wind.

a world arranged with grace

in a world arranged with grace,
where distant hills converge,
where flowers open near sun-dappled panes,
where weeds rise softly through soil,
where birds sing unseen above,
where turtles linger beneath hushed water,
where fallen branches lean into ponds,

sculpting shade and reflection,
where insects drift through panes of sun,
where butterflies turn the air yellow and white,
where trees unfold into true shapes,
where light and shadow linger in shared quiet,

there moves the single disturbance,
the tremor running crosswise through calm,
a pulse against the rhythm of leaf and shade.

footfalls scatter water into shifting rings,
steps against the shoal, nudging the quiet,
blinks breaking the seamless green hush,
thoughts a question unanswered, sending ripples
across the delicate balance.

i wish to vanish like winter,
brief, essential, then gone,
so the world might be untroubled by my frost,
so others might remain
in the symmetry of trees and shadows and summer,
unruffled by my discord,
untouched by my human shine, that restless gleam.

humid light

it is the brush rattling beneath the sun,
shifting to catch a breeze
in the heavy hushing of afternoon.
a blackbird fractures the moment,
all clang and startled wing,
while quieter birds persist,
scoring the distance in softer notes.

i pass the mural,
snow white in baby blue and pearl,
tilted against the concrete wall,
a white tube lifted to her nose,
eyes closed in cartoon bliss.
resting in heat and spray paint,
cradled in city sweat.

nearby, turtles stretch
beneath the wide glare of water.
wild flowers rise through gravel and chainlink,
purple against the rust.
dragonflies dart, yellow and flickering,
above the gleam of needle-drop boxes.

the idle youth lean back on benches,
their laughter, slow and blunt,
as the humidity softens their edges.
and still, kindness rises,
vapour in air,
from the asphalt, the lake, the wild, and the rust.

echoes of fragility

wave after wave,
even the calm sea will rage.
what are tides, what is sunshine,
when may falls wet upon the skin.

the body drifts from its anchor.
skin gathers quiet blooms.
the hand that once held fire
trembles with cracks, with time.

knuckles trace clay and memory.
the palm, etched in the grain of wood,
a ropeburn, a tender map
drawn in flesh and brine.

the tide turns in the marrow.
the sea offers soft passage.
it breaks and remakes.
each foam-lit swell, a reminder,
healing speaks in rhythm.

within the pull and push,
a shape begins to form,
drawn from the wound,
and the light that enters after.

the river

there is a river
older than me,
older than you,
wider than kingdoms,
deeper than the watchfulness of prayer.

it runs through the broken heart of the world,
through the cracked bones of cities,
through the dust where names sleep.

it carries banners of mercy,
it bears victories of the unseen.
it moves with tenderness that endures.

those who kneel to drink from it
taste the ancient sweetness of life,
that strength which rises through sorrow.

this river flows through every hand lifted in thirst,
this river begins in the heart of mercy,
this river carries all who surrender to its current.

i have fallen into it,
still, it bears.

i come to home

the blue should move me to tears.
currents,
clouds on clouds, folding into waves

rock of my bones.
shield and mountain.
keeper of what holds
when nothing else holds.

over and under the earth
you rise.
and i return.

i come to home through knowing,
through ease
and through bearing.
being carried
on shoulders and wings.

vasileion

the kingdom is like a grain of mustard seed.
attention must be steady,
must single it out,
it slips easily into the crevices of your palm, or drifts on the wind,
falling from the base of your wrist.

a grain is the grain.
one is all; all are in one.

hide it in three inches of earth.
tend to it,
wait as it breaks the surface,
a young seedling stretching for air.

there will be nesting birds
in its maturing branches,
and those branches hold your life.

ways of walking

i am a dying man, threading pine-shadowed paths,
under vaults of copper light breaking into shifting coins.
my steps crush resin's sharp perfume,
the hush older than marble, worn smooth by centuries of thought.

these trees train my gaze to lower,
to trace roots rising like questions from dark earth,
to feel branches lean and brush my forehead,
until even giants bow
to trunks older than our empires.

yet i am also a man who has walked among sunlit ruins,
where columns stand tall, hot beneath the sun,
casting ripples across my skin,
as the air quivers with heat and distant footfalls,
beneath a sky wide as thought,
where once scholars gathered from far cities,
speaking of virtue,
shaping measured words,
imagining lives lifted, like arches.

there, mined matter, shaped to math and symmetry,
directs me toward a sky pale as pergamena,
and my shoulders rise,
as if i too might claim the human shape
as measure, as compass point,
as the silent spine of pale sky.

in such places, the air is humid with human striving,
eroding memory into stone,
so thought might rise beyond the weight of flesh.

in the forest, the air quivers with pine needles and insect wings,
summoning me to stoop, to listen,
to dwell among things close to the ground.

i claim neither way as higher.
i walk both paths,
eyes lifted to parian glow,
lowered to trails braided with scent and shade.

i am learning how both ways of walking shape one path,
how the human heart stays stretched between sky and soil,
eyes wandering between heights and shadows,
each step tracing a line of grandeur and humility,
bearing the quiet question of where to turn my gaze.

the way a river changes

if i have changed,
it is in the way a river changes,
not by choice, but by erosion.

not the kind stamped and sealed,
not grade a eggs, not fresh bread,
but what gets filed under
the wrong funding codes,
what counts the cries in a ward,
what maps sorrow with precision.

if i speak of pain,
i mean the way a building hesitates
before becoming rubble.
the way an elder's name outlives
the mouth that spoke it.

if i have changed,
it is because i passed through all of it
and kept walking,
thinking of my sleep,
the hallway hum,
the latch catching in the night.

if i have changed,
it is because i lived beyond time,
losing days like coins
dropped into collection plates,
lighting candles
for the dead,
and for the living,
who wait in vestibules
between mass and absence.

if i carry mercy now,
it is because grace came unasked,
in the shape of sandwiches in paper bags,
in the voice of a stranger
who handed me water without questions,
who let me leave
before i learned their name.

if i have changed,
it is because i drifted
from hour to dusk,
from season to forgetting,
from youth to a mirror
that does not blink,
where even my eyebrows speak
of time.

if i have changed,
it is because i have begun
to carry beauty like a wound,
and hope
as if it might be taken from me.
and still,
i lift my hand
to touch the side of my face,
just to be sure
it is still me.

boundless

there are no borders, no outlines, to these days.

the maths oscillate
between one and countless,
visible, obscured,
collapsing inward, expanding through distance,
arrays forming, scattering,
vanishing before numbers
can hold their shape.

a fence, grain gone fibrous,
wood split and swollen,
boundaries thinning
into splinters and spaces,
lines once strict
now soft as worn thread.

darkness holds no shape.
it seeps through spans,
settles into hollows unmapped,
persists where measure
once imposed certainty.

there is light,
entire in itself,
threading subtle shifts,
low magnitudes,
fine scatterings across glass,
over etched metal,
along water's pale plane.

i stay within coordinates,
listening to frequencies
where even silence
leaves faint remains.

sometimes i wish
to view the world as a single speck,
minute enough to hover weightless,
held in the margin
where matter and energy
pause, poised between events.

i hold no refusal
against the flux,
no line against the chance
that illumination may reach here.

this perspective knows no confines.
nor does radiance.
both extend until shapes dissolve,
and in that haze,
i speak a quiet wish
that motion returns,
that smallest presences
find their bearings again
in the shifting array.

mercy in the frost

mercy is the hush of first snow,
settling without demand.
strength is the oak,
its branches scarred, still reaching.

i walk the morning fields,
the frost breaks under my step.
sparrows lift in sudden flight,
their wings a kind of hymn.

what falters in me is lifted,
what bends is steadied.
each silence opens into song,
each shadow thins with light.

teach me the patience of roots,
the endurance of rocks in rain.
let me lean into the day
as fields lean into weather.

and when the night comes down,
let me rest in its mercy,
let me wake in its strength,
held by what endures.

fresh as snow

the light is fresh as snow.
it rests on the morning dome,
a glaze of frost laid down in silence
through the night.
the sky is still so much morning
it has not yet turned blue.
it leans to rose,
as if the day itself were pausing
before choosing its color.

in the crest of the valley the sun peers through.
shrubs turn to glass, every twig shining
with a brittle gleam.
one tree rises above the others,
stretching toward the opposite ridge,
its trunk drawn upward,
its crown still half in shadow,
its whole form braced
between light and night.

higher on the bank
an evergreen catches the sun.
its branches grip their green,
dark and steady against the bright seam of the hill.
its roots press into the slope,
deep into the damp soil,
anchored as seasons circle around it.
it seems to stand as a column holds its place,
gathering years into its body
without a sound.

where water trickles over rock,
foam gathers white as ice.
the thin stream flashes in sudden brightness,
its edges silvered black with wet.
light lays itself there
as if no weight could disturb it,

while the current appears
to carry snow again,
fresh, unfallen,
the whole valley exuding light.

it is a new day

even boulders ground to sand,
pummelled by starlight,
eroded by foam and wind.

grain upon grain
of ancient mountains
broken, breaking still,
shaping new shifting landscapes
on the scales of giants.

beneath our cracked feet,
under a cracked sky,
the sun sets
in red and sombre shades.

we brush aside the ancients
as we brush sand from lashes and brows,
without reverence,
as if these were only seeds of wisdom
fallen on a winter's day.

some mornings

some mornings fracture beneath unseen weight,
molten rivers pressing upward, breaking through.
asphalt buckles, roads split open,
lines mapping the restless ground.

on these mornings, a touch lands heavy,
its weight neither tender nor cruel.
words strike, glances cut.
we rise from tangled sheets
raw as rocks lifted from fire.

these mornings call for love,
love pressed into us like roots in rock,
slow, steady, unrelenting.
it shapes us as crystals are shaped,
compressed into edge,
their light born from strain.

love moves molten, flowing toward us,
bright and alive, cooling in place,
a thin crust hardening where it spreads.
step carefully. it will hold
yet fractures under sudden weight.

morning splits open, light seeping
through seams thinned by the night.
roots twist deeper, taking hold.
the day waits, raw as cooling magma,
soft enough to keep our mark.

threads of flight

brown moth,
your flight threads the air,
each flutter sewing silence,
each arc lifting the weight of stillness.
your wings, dusk-colored and thin,
skim through shadows beyond reach,
folding seen and unseen
into the hush of their motion.

each beat shakes loose fruit swelling unseen,
seed pressed under soil,
flour dusting the hands that knead.
you move where labor bends into grace,
where silence holds what words cannot shape.
your wings stir dust from forgotten rooms,
the lines of faces creased by wind and time,
each wrinkle an echo rising.

we follow your trembling course,
a fragile arc through the vast,
crossing thresholds unnamed.
light reaches,
singeing your span,
igniting the air with its grip.
every rise carries hunger,
the glow irresistible as the shadow it casts.

the flame, both haven and fire,
warmth and undoing.
your wings drive on,
their rhythm alive with grace
even as the light consumes.
the air bends, the flame lifts,
and still you climb.

brown moth,
you are flight along the edge of loss,

the bearer of what slips the grasp.
you rise toward a burning
that summons all who chase it,
a thread between ash and morning,
between ember and sky.

even as the flame takes you,
even as your wings turn to ash,
this is your flight,
lifted for a moment,
as a shadow called to light.

how we build the light

designs do not rise from rows of cells.
they begin where earth gives way to the plow,
where the forge glows red with heat,
the hymn of hands,
working toward what cannot yet be seen.

systems murmur where we gather,
chalk-sketches of song carried into morning light.
plasticine bends to dreams,
air thickens with thought,
shaping what waits to take form.

every number is a whisper,
every cell a spark, unlit
until the touch of fire and wind.
classrooms stretch beyond their dividers,
beams extending like arms to the sky.
each seat holds more than a body,
it holds a mind, a question, a flame.

the monk's trembling screen bears more
than the flicker of words.
it carries life, still warm,
edges curling toward the open.
what we craft are baskets, yes,
but not for dimming,
for carrying.

we carry flames to the hilltop,
to the sea's edge,
waiting for light.
this is how we build:
in sparks, in steps,
in hands that never stop
shaping the air.

the light between us

we sit together in the soft afternoon,
decades collapsing gently around us.
your voice carries stories
that ripple like a stream,
touching moments we both remember,
and some I can only imagine.

your laugh blooms,
a sound that feels like sunlight,
spilling warmth across the room.
we share a glance, unspoken,
as if the years between
were never quite separate.

your hands rest lightly,
their lines soft reminders
of paths traveled,
each a quiet testament
to days that built this moment.

there's nothing heavy here,
only the sweet weight of presence,
of being here, together,
with no need to hurry
or chase what has passed.

we linger in the golden light,
time stretching itself kindly.
this is the gift we share.
the joy of simply being,
of knowing that right now
is everything we need.

winter love

smell sweetly,
my sweet, of french roses, of jasmine.
orangeries and perfumeries seek you,
alchemy and nature bow
as you pass.

you are woman,
ancient wisdom,
and sweet things unspoken.
honey, perhaps,
or something subtler,
more profound.

even duress cannot dim you.
of all things,
most sweetly,
be.

rest day

i will rest today,
let the day make progress elsewhere.
time can be layered above me,
like branches heavy with shade.

to rest feels like words unformed,
a voice held in the chest.
there is sadness in this quiet,
a longing to fill the hours with motion,
but the stillness carries its own music,
a sound only heard
when the world slows.

this is the shape of what is right.
to step aside from the rushing stream,
to sit at its edge,
watching shadows break and rejoin,
feeling the weight of the moment settle.

dreams bloom in the pause,
visions carried gently on the breeze,
thoughts untethered,
wandering toward distant skies.
to rest is to gather these fragments,
to weave them into something whole.

i will rest today,
and the day will carry me softly,
its quiet a cradle,
its tranquility a hymn.
in the sadness, clarity,
a brief sense of rightness,
the rightness of yielding
to what the body and spirit ask.

seven suns

there were seven suns,
each born of a different mother,
sharing the sky's shifting
from blue into white.

the first sun, pale and gaunt,
walked into the early hours
like a ghost returning home.
his glow pressed thin against the earth,
a blur on cold glass, fading as it formed.
in his time, silence gathered,
and those who rose searched for his shadow
in the hollows of grit and frost.

the second sun followed,
slipping in between sleep and waking.
his warmth rose and ebbed,
as unpredictable as water brushing a shore.
some mornings, his light held laughter.
other mornings, it tasted of words
held tight in the jaw.

the third sun leapt upward,
scattering gold like grain across the land.
his rays stretched wide and bright,
reaching into every hollow,
every crevice,
as though to strip the last trace of dark.
his laughter spilled over fields and rivers,
hungry to carve his name in light.

the fourth sun moved
with a craftsman's care,
steady as a wheel on its axle.
his illumination carried no haste,
only a rhythm that guided
fields into furrow,
hands into work,

boulders struck to form.
his was the hour of balance,
where nothing hurried
and nothing slept.

the fifth sun stepped heavy with color,
his light thinning
along the rim,
a red on the edge of breaking.
he painted air in fading hues,
each one fragile at day's edge.
his presence carried
the sting of endings,
beauty holding ground
until the light thinned away.

the sixth sun flickered
at the seam of day and night,
his glow shattering,
scattering like fireflies
over darkening fields.
restless with urgency,
he trembled at time's pull,
burned only to sting the air,
then gave way.

the seventh sun did not rise.
he lived within the dark,
unseen but certain,
his hours folding like cloth laid flat,
covering the sky in rest.
under his watch,
shadows held their ground,
and the world exhaled.
his presence was a pause,
gathering strength
until eyes lifted again
to the first sun.

thick with light

the night clung like oil,
its breath damp in the corners,
each fold of darkness stretched taut,
a silence steeped in waiting.

a thread of gold pulled loose
from shadow's weave,
its edge sharp,
its warmth rising,
pressed against the skin.

on the floor, it traced
the grain of wood,
each plank swelling with gold,
veins glinting like rivers
splitting the surface.

the air turned vivid,
layered with brightness
that opened hollow spaces to glow.
folds stretched wide,
swelling with color,
flames rising slow
from embers.

fingers broke the surface of the glow,
their tips streaked with fire.
heat coursed beneath the skin,
trails of brightness etched deep,
a shimmer that lingered like memory.

the room became a canvas,
its walls painted in motion,
shapes undone and remade
as brilliance spilled outward.
light wove the world larger,
its edges alive,
unraveling into radiance.

the air carried its shimmer,
its pulse thickened every moment.
corners unfurled,
each surface alive.

the room swelled outward,
dissolved in an amber tide.
light spilled its weight into air,
a pulse expanding,
each moment shaped anew,
a world opened
into bloom.

as water moves

the tent opened wide,
its canvas pulled apart,
ropes straining in the morning air.
the cloth smelled of dust and rope,
its seams tight with waiting.
inside, the air thickened,
a hush pressed close to the skin,
as though the ground itself
was holding its sound.

voices gathered,
low, uneven,
rising and breaking,
one over another.
words spilled forward,
layering like water against cliffs.

the noise moved as water moves,
steady, without seam,
settling against everything it met.
its reach was gentle,
its warmth quiet

first hour

the first hour steadies the morning through labour.

its poems mark the gestures of work, the ordering of the body, and the discipline of attention.

this is the hour of folding, mending, and lifting, where small acts become prayer when carried with care.

the reader is invited to enter the day through these tasks, to feel the morning shaped by labour offered with devotion.

mercy in the morning

there is mercy in the morning light,
forgiveness the bed cannot grant.
the dark loosens,
and its breaking is strange,
eleusinian,
so we watch,
seeking balance for the soul.

the floorboards creak.
i limp from here to there,
until light clears my eyes
of the weight of last night
and the nights before.

enter light into my mouth,
make my tongue a psalm,
so i might sing a hallelujah.

reasons i fold my clothes in silence

because sound might undo
what little shape the day has taken,
sitting hunched between the dryer and the air exchange.

a shirt, a towel, a pair of socks,
brought into rough symmetry.

because i once watched
someone i loved
fold a shirt along its seams,
as if it were a wound
that could be closed.
they pressed with joy,
imprinting order on a wrinkled world.

because silence
is the only fabric
that does not fray.

because i want to remember
how a sweater holds warmth,
even after the body is gone.

because the drawer
is a kind of grave,
with a sour smell like turned earth,
and everything deserves
a soft burial.

inventory of threadbare things

where shall we rest for a moment
in this loneliness,
which is the world
thinned to a single thread.

thread upon thread,
knot upon knot,
each crooked, unfinished,
the trace of a making we cannot see.

what shall i do
with my solitary heart,
my unshaven youth,
its face bent toward the cold.

what hunger hollowed the chest,
what grief sifted its marrow,
leaving this body laid open,
a feast for the crows at dawn.

day to day

before speech, before reckoning, all pressed within all.
depth without edge, weight without measure,
the whole held in its fullness.
a word struck. the break tore through fullness,
driving light from lightlessness,
casting each to its place, pushing them apart.
light surged.
darkness yielded, pulled to its measure.
they met at the edge, testing their reach.
morning rose, evening gathered behind.
the world gasped. time poured through the opening,
the first measure laid down,
a count set in the shape of division.
evening came, and morning,
and the first day stood.

a word struck. the deep split apart.
a vault rose, lifting weight from weight,
holding the upper flood in its mass,
binding the depths within their reach.
the sky braced against the waters above,
kept them in place, bore them in silence.
below, the flood swayed within its command,
set to the spoken-for limits.
another word.
the firmament stood,
the heights carried their burden,
the depths bore their measure.
evening came, and morning,
and the second day stood.

a word struck. the flood gathered itself.
earth bracing against earth,
ridges lifted, valleys settled into their reach.
waters withdrew, drawn toward the spaces set for them.
another word. soil gripped the roots,
branches reached upward,
seed bore seed, branch bore branch.
growth filled the world, rising as it was spoken.

the land stood.
the waters held.
the command stood firm.
evening came, and morning,
and the third day stood.

a word struck. fire lit.
flame caught flame and set upon its course.
heat bored, shadows thinned,
rivers gathered light, the earth turned,
as if turning in sleep beneath it.
another word. a lesser light took hold,
lifting the tides, bearing the night.
its face turned, full, empty, carrying time.
another word. the stars burned into the firmament,
placed beyond reach,
set to reckon the days,
measuring turning upon turning.
the count gathered.
day bore its name, the night its weight.
the world turned, turning,
bound to the course set for it.
evening came, and morning,
and the fourth day stood.

a word struck then poured into the depths.
life bore through the waters, multiplying,
filling the spaces within them.
another word. wings unfurled like masts in haste,
lifting into the firmament,
striking against the wind.
the air held its charge,
the waters bore their fullness.
another word. they multiplied,
carried the word spoken into them.
waters surged, and sky withstood the weight of motion.
evening came, and morning,
and the fifth day stood.

a word struck.
limb, sinew, claw, hoof.
the land bore its charge,

flesh came forth, life carried through the body.
hunger drove them, movement swept them outward,
the quick and the heavy, the great and the hidden,
each driven toward its course, filling the world.
another word.
limbs braced, hands reached.
this one stood.
the first to measure.
the first to shape.
the first to press meaning into the earth.
beasts surged ahead,
scattered through grasses,
raced through rivers,
vanished into trees.
they would pass, and land
would not carry them.
this one.
this one pressed words into dust.
evening came, and morning,
and the sixth day stood.

a word struck,
and the speaking ceased.
another word, held within the formed.
rivers gathered their charge,
their paths waiting for other hands.
trees bore their fruit,
those who gathered pressed names into them.
stars turned and glittered,
their count awaiting reckoning.
making continued.
it carried on.
words shaped the dust.
the charge remained.
those shaped by it
stood within the world,
bearing the charge of shaping.
evening came, and morning,
and the seventh day stood.

storm door soprano

you stand at the storm door
the one we defied, ignoring each murmur of warning.
glass pressed to steel, a union neither safe nor simple,
yet it holds us, and the house,
and the morning that enters unbidden.

light pools on your shoulders.
your bare feet find the cool tile.
you lean, a whisper,
to linger with the garden's slow becoming.
the hanging baskets sway like quiet bells
in green profusion.

you watch unvoiced,
your silence considered.

from the hallway the music lifts
a passage we once left behind,
the second movement left unplayed.

i recall the airport's glass
the sky a fractured mosaic
the plane's indifferent climb.
and here only the voice
a pure ascending thread.

i wait apart
where the morning's melody is softer.
no need for touch
no call for words.

you are whole in this light.
you are already complete.
and my love,
forged through fire and quiet weariness,
now softened in the hush of your becoming,
sheds its intricate folds
within your stillness,
where even the air begins to sing.

the same stone

a lion bends,
shoulders broad, waist drawn tight,
black stone gleaming, muscles wound deep,
a body twisting from the strike.

hands pressed weight into marble,
chiseling sorrow into the jaw,
power into the back,
turning stone to something heaving.

a mane spills,
pain opens the face, carved in muscle,
pressed into the ribs, into the eyes,
where the wound pauses before the roar.

strength remains.
even as it turns,
rage moves slow,
grief dense as dusk settling,
power rooted in the frame.

from this stone rises the figure,
shoulders drawn, sorrow seated deep,
cut from the same unyielding weight.
doubt lives in the curve of a shoulder,
reluctance in the turn of retreat.

the sculptor carved lion and body together,
grief pressed into the form,
rage set in the spine,
time carved into the eyes.

even as the form turns away,
it is taking shape,
a figure wrought by struggle,
a presence waiting to rise.

intercostal

my heart is flat as the day,
grey since morning.
grey like the ache in my back,
the intercostal pull threading the ribs,
tightening as it inspires,
waiting before it returns.

this day is black,
dimmed by a sun that hides in masquerade.

grey upon grey.
this day will pass
as all days pass,
grey upon grey.

receive even this difficult day.
it is only time
until the deeper pain returns.
you cannot make the pain obey.

so i drink these bitter drops.
so i drink to the bottom of the cup.

day by day.
day by day by day.

askizometha

we break, and the earth opens,
her veins spilling darkness,
heavy with isotopes,
elements forged in the crush of stars.

time shatters, brilliance scattering
near the edge of an event horizon.
hands fractured by the force,
fingers trembling in the light's slow flood.

spirals tighten, galaxies rip their centres,
their symmetry carved in collapse.
fields of dust harden like glass,
their echoes pressing against the membrane of time.

beneath the vast silence of night,
beginnings splinter.
from splinters of brilliance, symmetry emerges,
igniting what sleeps in the bellies of the stars.

orion stretches across space like a wound,
his belt trembling in the pull of distance,
filaments of light stitched into the fabric,
a map traced for one who seeks,
perhaps for something remembered,
or for what drifts beyond memory.

the earth tilts on an axis,
its rhythm murmuring softly,
leaves shuffle in the air.
a gyroscope spins mid-flight,
holding balance in the promise of its fall.

redshift deepens the heavens,
light stretches as it flees,
its colour shifting,
each wave a record of what once was.
stars recede, their stories thinning,
leaving the echo of their motion.

a comet veers into its arc,
dust trailing like forgotten vows.
its curve holds gravity's ancient hymn,
its path older than the first word spoken into fire.

hips grind fossils into motion,
each joint a millstone turning slow,
singing in the marrow of the body,
its gears caked with centuries of ash.

relief seeps,
thick as resin,
into the grain of skin.
a pact forged in nerve and sinew,
the body holding its erosion at bay.

memory sharpens itself,
a mother's warmth fossilised in bone.
the curve of her arms,
once a cradle for my body,
now a hollow pressed into my ribs.

pain charts its rivers into flesh,
a delta carving tributaries of ache.
scars pool in quiet hollows,
feeding the still ocean that rises in the dark,
pulled by unseen weights.

love's decay radiant and slow.
like light moving through water,
its spectrum stretches through years,
reaching for what was held, then gone.

the hand remembers its quiet language,
its weight folding softly into ribs,
carving absence into a shelter.

the earth turns through collisions,
each tilt a scar carved in stone,
her axis forged in the heat of impact.
the ground holds its ache in quiet bones.

my body curls again, as if remembering
her warmth, the cradle of her arms.
the balance of stillness and motion
woven into a gesture older than stars.

orion stretches across the stillness,
his shoulders, hips, arms marking time's compass,
each thread trembling with memory.

balance teeters on the gyroscope's tilt,
its spin promising what cannot hold.

all things fold toward resolution.
stars draw inward,
a comet trailing arcs of dust and distance.
we, too, bend into this pull,
an unseen gravity gathering us whole,
forging the scatter of our beginning into form.

deal with the universe

make a deal with the universe.
it will take what it can.
it will press you low,
put your hands in the dirt,
turn your face from the sky.

but the ground is not a grave,
and sorrow is not the end.

it will pull you down,
but it cannot keep you there.
no, it cannot keep you there.
it will pull you down,
but it cannot keep you there.

there's a cost to inhaling,
there's a price on hope.
but you rise with the morning,
you rise when it's time.
every time.

the ground is not a grave,
sorrow is not the end,
pull down, rise up.

the sky is waiting
when the story's told.

the universe will pull you down,
but it cannot keep you there.
that is the deal we have made.

clinamen

the world arrived   without decree.
one atom swerved
as it fell
and direction
took form.

this is why
there is motion.
why weight
leans into shape.
why nothing
holds still.

before speech,
there was contact.
before design,
the drift.

a man once said
we are made
of the same dust
as the stars.

he meant to console.
i mean to describe.

third hour

the third hour opens to fire and inspiration.

the poems in this section lean into vision, imagination, and the sudden spark of the spirit.

it is the hour of voices, of figures drawn from memory and tradition, of flames that illuminate both mind and heart.

here the reader enters the wide field of thought and breathes in the force that sustains it.

parvati and the gull

i did not ask for resurrection.
if i did, the mind was elsewhere.
i recall sitting with parvati.

wind crossing the sunlit gravel.
the light falling as if it had weight.
a crystal sky above.

the waves performed a ballet.
today they still do.
yellow and itching,
the skin warm as bruised fruit.
the body a lip at the edge of an abyss,
dark water pressing its cold mouth to the rock.
my hands cupped around the air.
as if it could be carried to safety.

instead i remained.
counting time as if it were coins.

i could give up the pita and cheddar.
the ravens lay them at my bed each dawn.
their wings black as questions.
their beaks precise as knives.
above them the same pale sky
where a gull wheels slowly,
marking the day in widening circles.
perhaps the ravens laugh when they leave.
i could open my sores to the air.
and name each one after a forgotten saint.

feathers turned like falling leaves.
the air ashen and metallic,
as if the sea had been poured through iron.

parvati listened.
her gaze pressed into the shoreline.
as though it were a thread.
held between two fingers.
the thread darkened in her hands.
she did not look away.

the wind tasted of sun.
and of something rising.
as if the waters
lift the light from their depths.
to make a body from what it touched,
its skin shining as if newly made.

waking or sleeping.
all is a beautiful lament.
pushed away by wind and sun.
danced into the glitter of waves.
the sea does not keep what it touches.
the shore does not keep what it loses.

a gull drifted over us.
its shadow brushed my cheek.
the cold tide touched my feet.
parvati's eyes followed the bird.
perhaps the gull mocked me.
mocked the yellowing and abyss.
her silence shifted in the wind.

let me be loved

let me be loved, my lord,
as morning light settles low across the field,
before dew beads along the stems,
before the crow calls once from the fence line.
i stand where night thins to pale
and the day's first warmth seeps into my fingers.

seedheads brittle, blades still keep their dust,
yellow weeds paper-bright through the summer's dry,
green clover close to the soil and cool,
ants crossing furrows in narrow lines,
and my shoulders draw in for rain.

let me come toward you,
as birch leaves turn to the first light.
white bark flares where the sun touches,
small pale tremors through the leaves.

i have walked long distances in sleep,
through rooms with doors i cannot open.
i wake on cracked soil veined with fine fissures,
my mouth dry with regret, my hands agape.

i have kept watch at bedsides in rooms of white light
and carried names home when monitors fell silent.
my steps shortened on the long walk home,
and i sat with my head bowed in the late blue of the windows.
days hung like heavy cloth on the shoulders.
i count what remains and what passes
and want the steadiness of quartz in place of dread.

i welcome the day you give.
i claim no right over light or wind.
i step into the hours as sunlight edges across the floor.
i keep to mercy for measure and pace.
the day's first warmth seeps deeper into my fingers,
as the morning settles lower across the field.

fearsome love

this is a fearsome and ancient love,
like eros, who stoked desire and dread alike.
he is the greeks' divine terror,
his arrows tipped with both fire and poison.

it is a broken love,
misshapen as a dog-chewed toy,
baked by sun, hard as ice on impact,
and fragile still,
splintering under the weight of its own longing.

it is also whole,
swollen by hope and forgiveness,
sutured like torn flesh,
monstrous in its parts,
reckoning weakness as courage.
this love is wrapped in soft things and multiple lights
to insulate against despair.

it is a fearsome love,
a love of howls and moaning.
in fear of god, we reckon divinity
in this shattered completeness.
we douse ourselves in fire,
worship at a flame,
burn like hunger in this conflagration of love.

love bends like fire,
dancing to the wind's direction,
feeding on the smallest fragments.
splinters, threads, the ache of a wick.
it rises, consuming itself in hunger,
until all that remains is its heat,
its light,
and the infinite, silent dark.

here i was, playing socrates.
but the answer is to become pure flame.

gregory's flame

i rise through matter
by motion alone.
each gesture opens
into the next,
lifting heat upward
in a single direction.

i dwell in ascent,
in brightness that turns
and leaves no ash.
my presence gathers
as invitation.

you arrived carrying a name,
spoken slowly,
as if it might take root.
you placed it down
among the folds of smoke,
where clarity bends into glow.

i draw all that turns toward me.
i meet the gaze
that stays open.
each step forms
in the act of reaching.
flame shapes its path by motion.

i pass through form
and leave it unchanged.
still you follow,
you reach.
you rise.

the heraclitean god

i speak in flame.
each word enters the air
and leaves it changed.
language forms
as a movement through heat,
never resting in sound.

you stepped into water
as it turned.
the river carried your shape
and left its pattern behind.
you felt motion
take hold.

i remain in change.
each moment completes
by passing into the next.
each form arrives once
and continues forward
with precision.

you shape granite into temples.
i release heat into matter.
you gather,
trace,
preserve.
i scatter.

you bring prayer
to what endures.
i mcct it
in turning.
your stillness draws flame
as it begins to change.

empedoclean

smoke blackens brick, swallowing light.
soot thickens on the walls,
air heavy with residue,
the ground still hot beneath its crust.

who begins the fracture,
the voice that carries itself into flame.
whispers dissolve into ash,
marble cracks against its own weight,
silence presses close.

would you leap into the red bloom.
the earth might close behind you.

fire cuts like a sculptor's hand,
light carved from stone.
its mercy swift, its patience only becoming.
love and strife spin the wheel,
clay rising under steady pressure.
molten rivers flow with the weight of change.
beneath your feet the ground heaves upward,
its promise total.

ash crumbles underfoot,
doubt remade in flame.
you see your name uncoil,
letters melted back into their oldest form.

before the leap, the body waits,
a hand gripping the ledge,
lungs holding a final thread of air.
desire swells, heat gathers at your heels,
fire speaking in the tongue of stars,
a memory pushed forward into shape.

there is no grief here,
only the pull of something ancient,
older than light, deeper than weight.
to surrender is to step into rhythm,
where flesh opens to flame.

in fire you are unmade,
folded open like smoke turning on itself.
flame cuts to the marrow,
its heat becomes your voice,
its glow your unbroken shape.
it lifts what once was heavy into air,
stripping away the long wait.

leap because silence yields nothing.
leap because fire holds
what the world lets go.
glory bends here,
where fire takes flesh into itself,
where the self burns into light.

what rises from flame is a life returned,
a spark spun into the hymn of stars,
burning where dark begins again.

see the moon

i did not see the moon,
which makes it difficult to judge
if we are waxing or waning,
blue or silver, bearing the sun's borrowed fire.

i could not see the hand before my eyes,
darker than the corner behind the bed,
creaking as if the old boilers still heaved below,
flames licking the brick in the basement.

i could not hear my thoughts.
they slipped like smoke,
pooled behind my skull,
while my heart beat against my jaw and teeth.

it comes this way each season:
in winter with the windows tight shut,
the heat ticking through the pipes,
in spring when the rain soaks the sill,
in summer with the air so dry
it scrapes the throat raw,
in autumn when leaves skitter the roof
and the nights fall early.
always the same rush,
the body braced for what never breaks.

here it is, the darkness.
here again, the familiar return.
cradle yourself in prayers, boy.
limp your way to bed.

petrarch's garden

do you know how gardens hold
the press of hands, how they bloom
in cities of glass and shadow,
each seed a promise pressed into soil.

i have walked where roses bend,
where light rests on every petal.
the air thick with pollen and sap,
each step a hymn to what might rise.

roses root deep as though the earth
took in every touch of love.
branches thorned and fragile
twist upward into sunlit air.

to tend is to scrape mud from your nails,
to bleed a little when the thorn resists,
to cut with care, knowing the rose
bears the mark of every hand.

petals fall and darken into soil,
their color feeding the root.
the night covers what will return,
spring held beneath the frost.

the sun leans close,
dew gathers clear on the leaves.
for a moment the garden glimmers,
a prayer caught in morning light.

there is no map here,
only paths worn by wandering.
each bloom fades, roots endure,
drawing us deeper into what is hidden.

love grows wild, unbound,
through cracks in the ground,
its fragrance lingering in silence,
its roots threading forgotten ground.

roses bear rain, the hush of frost,
the long patience of winter.
yet they rise again, their petals bright,
their beauty risen from earth.

as petrarch bowed to his roses,
we bow to love that lingers still,
hands dirtied in devotion,
hearts open, always growing.

between the apocalypses

i went for a walk, shaky and slow,
from the market to the bookshop,
stopping for flowers,
stooping to smell.

before the first of the apocalypses,
i went for a mineral bath,
stretching out in epsom with lavender smell,
in steaming waters,
in swirling thought.

after the second of the apocalypses,
i groaned for an hour,
rubbing my heel,
lamenting my timing,
which was characteristic

and out of tune
with the music in all those steps.

we are those summer leaves

we are those summer leaves
strewn across the yard in early autumn.
the sun still stands high,
and one may walk to the water's edge
without the weight of a coat.

we are the late sea,
with minerals heavy on its tongue,
anemones fastened to rocks.
its surface gathers light
even as the days draw in,
each wave carrying weight and release,
each crest folding back into itself.

we are chipmunks in quiet gardens,
clambering through hanging pots,
cheeks swollen with seed.
their hidden labor reshapes the season,
a storehouse built
from what is nearly gone.

these are the brief things,
the signs of living that pass quickly.
they rest closer than dispute,
truer than the lists that divide our days.
to hold them is to carry the season entire,
its nearness pressed into the hand.

open field

in the open field,
a single tree leans into the sky,
its branches stretched wide,
catching the slow crawl of clouds.
it stands between the rolling and flat landscapes,
a quiet sentinel,
its shadow falling over time itself.

like me, walking alone and together,
rooted in silences shared
with memories,
or perhaps with no one at all.
the sky stretches on, vast and endless,
and the wind carries whispers I cannot place.
but I walk.

in this life,
even solitude leaves its mark,
like roots breaking open the earth.
the tree holds the weight of storms,
its shadow bends with the sun.
and I too, keep moving,
both reaching and still,
knowing the open field is its own kind of home.

salt thick on the tongue

the streets are sodden,
windows blur with the long rain.
night hangs swollen with weeping,
its threads caught on the eaves.

the streets darken under the downpour,
lamps flicker and vanish,
water runs hard along the gutters,
a silence gathers behind the rain.

this is the hour that delivers us,
the hour that demands we rise.
we go out anyway,
salt burning the palms,
the mouth thick with storm.

each step strikes the black road,
each step a blunt refusal.
we keep moving into the dark,
the body a lantern, lit by sweat,
held steady against the wind.

lost beyond the path

the track I followed broke apart,
its lines erased by falling light.
I searched for its trace,
but shadow covered shadow,
and the ground offered only silence.

each step thinned to nothing,
each turn led back to thicket and night.
what I had called a way
was only a clearing,
a moment's order among branches.

dark closed in,
and I stood where direction failed,
carried by the hush of leaves
and the faint scent of earth cooling after day.

the weight

i cry out, but the echo returns,
longer, stretched by the stone-throat of the wall.
this darkness has measured my days,
has counted my ribs as a guard marks the hours.

i have known saints who burned,
who bent beneath iron, who knelt in dust.
they whispered into the wind,
and still, the wind did not answer.

o lord, you have set this weight on me.
if this is the path, if this is the shaping,
know this: i am worn smooth.

a blade grinds itself to silence after so many sharpenings.
a vessel glows before the fire withdraws.
press your hand on me,
for i am wind-scattered, spent.

if this is the shaping, let it carve deep.
let it press until something answers.
let the weight settle, let it teach.
let the fire rise, stripping the husk.
let the night hold its ember.

i have been given to the flame,
and i rise in the glow.
i have been pressed as a weight upon the earth,
and my shape remains
as quietude deepens.

i die daily

i heard their stories first in the hush of evening,
on my mother's lap where her voice wove flame and silence.
the martyrs stood in fire, hands lifted, unbreaking,
lips shaping names before dawn.

she spoke of swords as garlands,
of iron and flame as love's bright ornaments.
in my child's heart i longed for such an end,
a spark flaring, a cry splitting dark.

their blood ran red as autumn's embers,
their bones bright relics of a world remade.
i thought of glory as the moment of burning,
the rise of the soul as the body fell away.

once i dreamed of rome and its open gates,
the stillness of sand before the lion's leap,
the ring of steel, the shout of the crowd,
the cry of the fallen fierce and free.

i would have walked into fire unshaken,
thrown my name like a banner to the wind,
stood as the blade bit through the silence,
if only to wear the laurel of the slain.

o childhood dream, bright as goldleaf,
soft as wax on the altar's edge.
it saw the beauty of an ending
but never the weight of beginning.

no fire came, no iron, no sudden severing,
only the slow press of morning on morning,
the weight of waiting, fingers curled cold,
silence held hard in the mouth.

no crown,
only the shaping of words,
the steadying hand.

to live in the offering, not in the moment of loss,
to wake in the thin light of morning, stretch into day,
to leave no mark, no monument carved,
only the space where self once stood.

the cup is full in the hands of the quiet,
the ones who pour out and never name it,
who wake before dawn and walk,
who light the lamp but do not linger.

not a life laid down but a life laid bare,
hands worn smooth by waiting,
a name thinned by silence on the tongue
in the moment of pause before speaking.

they are the ones who stand unseen,
who let the work speak in its own voice,
who carry the burden and call it no weight.

i heard hagiography first in the hush of evening,
small hands against hers, the still of a room.
i thought it was fire, but now i know
it is the thought held back, the step retaken.

no sudden blaze, no single cry,
only the long, slow turning toward light.
to die daily, to rise again, to give and not gather,
to wear the earth thin with the rhythm of going.

oblate poet

come, sadness,
come, burden of days.
wash me in grief,
lay me down in silence.

come, longing,
come, shadowed fire.
press me into the crystal,
where words strike sparks.

the muses rise in tears,
their hymn a slow river of ore.
their offering is weeping,
their gift poured out in silence.

i give myself to this weight,
to poisons that sharpen the tongue,
to wounds that open the voice.
i become the vessel,
emptied,
and the song endures.

down to the ice

i was downcast on the ice,
slipped and struck,
the crack of bone against frozen earth.
pain had not yet rooted itself,
only the knife's shadow waiting for blood.
i was shaken by the tremor in my legs,
ashamed at the falter i followed.

down to the rock-ice, cold in its grip.
down to the pavement, swallowing sound.
down to the hidden water, frozen veins below.
down to the iron, bones of the city.
down to the soil, roots twisted in clay.
into the hush, where no step can echo.
down to the bone, marrow ringing with cold.

i muttered into the cold air,
watching myself from a distance,
as if i were both the condemned
and the one who passed the sentence.

and the shame,
the ice clung to it and amplified it,
sharpening its edge like glass
as pain rose in waves through the body.

up through the marrow, still ringing with cold.
up through the bone, aching yet whole.
up through the hush, silence lifting its weight.
up through the soil, roots threading their hold.
up through the iron, bones of the city stirring.
up through the water, its echo returned.
up through the rock-ice, its grip splintering.

up through the chest, pulse carrying weight.
up through the throat, a cry pressed to silence.
up through the mouth, steam breaking to air.
into the air, where nothing can hold it.
up to the sky, blank and listening.
up to the silence, wide as the frozen ground,
cold and unbroken.

i was lifted from the frozen ground,
stood and shaken,
yet the body bore me upward,
and i walked on,
step after step into the cold.

palpitation

i saw nothing of the moon.
the sky closed its mouth, swallowed its teeth,
left no trace of waxing or waning,
no blue sheen, no silver scar.

i reached for my hand and found only air,
dense as the hush of a sealed room,
the floorboards groaning,
iron glowing in the belly of the house.

thoughts scattered beyond their borders.
the heart struck upward into the jaw,
hammered the teeth,
echoed against the tongue.

here it comes, the darkness.
here again, its slow collapse.
i gather myself in prayer,
while the limp shadows every step.

then a faint light widened,
not enough to name,
only the suggestion of a circle
loosening its hold on the dark.

endoscope

the sky opened in striations
of silver, white, and blue.
the snow has receded.
the grass remains, improbable,
green, brown, and yellow,
clinging at winter's margin,
rooted between pebble and slush.

its colour seems borrowed
from another season.
no green elsewhere,
only these thin veins,
pressed into cold earth,
holding as ice withdraws.

and the sky opened in striations,
light breaking through like lace,
and my heart was traced likewise,
lined with light, with ice,
each vessel visible,
the muscle lit from within.

tidewater

tidewater erases its own margin,
writing, unwriting,
the script of return.

coastlines flicker and thin,
names scattered like shells
crushed under the swell.

i am fault lines and floodplain,
a map redrawn each season,
its fractures filling with water,
its borders dissolving in silt.

layers settle into silence,
each deposit a verse laid down,
a liturgy of passage,
spoken once, then carried away.

the tide chants in a tongue without memory,
each surge a sentence erased in its echo,
each retreat an amen
that waits for its reply.

and still it carries me,
salt on the mouth,
a weight that does not loosen,
a promise kept by constancy of tides.

altar of frost

the morning is an altar of frost,
snow hardened by wind's sharp edge,
light scattered in specks, a fleeting gospel
written in ice, for one day alone.

the cul-de-sac glitters, its jewels dissolve;
the sun will rise, and its heat will unmake
this fragile scripture of night.

yet shadow lingers where light retreats,
its touch soft, its depth healing.
what seems absent fills the air unseen.

peter's shadow moved like a veil,
falling over the sick and broken;
chains broke, grace whispered,
loosening the bindings of the flesh.

the frost vibrates with silence,
each crystal a hymn refracting the sun.
this stillness, this darkness before the day,
holds secrets etched in fragile light.

i step outside, and the air clings,
sharp and holy, a baptism of cold.
the road, half-paved in frost and snow,
leads somewhere only light and shadow know.

the shadow waits beyond the frost,
its darkness bears only fullness.
will it pass over me too, and heal,
binding together what lies undone.

on the snow's surface, tracks of birds,
a fleeting text that will fade by noon.
their steps echo a quieter grace,
written briefly, then lifted to the heavens.

the walls of the cell are stiff and taciturn,
but prayer rises like warmth in winter.
won't an angel visit this narrow space,
its light unspoken but wholly present.

chains press close; yet within them,
a holiness stirs, forged in longing.
the weight of iron teaches the soul
how to wait for hands unseen.

an angel's light falls quiet as frost,
piercing into caves, unmaking the chains.
the shadow of wings lingers behind,
guiding the prisoner into the open night.

even in silence, shadows move,
stretching across the frost.
their weight carries the memory of healing,
a brush of grace that lingers unseen.

each day begins like this frost,
hard-edged and brilliant,
its brilliance a gift, its brevity a reminder
that eternity hides in the fleeting.

the road stretches, lit and veiled,
each path a story unfolding.
light led peter, shadow followed,
each step holy in its weight.

the chains fall without a sound,
dissolving like frost under sunlight.
grace moves unseen, quiet as sleep,
working deep beneath the surface.

prisoner and healer, bound and free,
these are the twin truths of grace,
etched in frost, cast in shadow,
a story whispered in the brief light of winter.

evening will come, and with it, rest.
the frost will harden again,
the shadow deepening, a quiet promise
that morning waits beyond the veil.

light and shadow entwine,
a dance eternal, neither one undone.
the snow glitters as a fleeting gift,
the shadow heals as an everlasting grace.

the day closes as it began,
with frost, with light, with mystery.
the chains of yesterday dissolve,

and tomorrow rises, halcyon and whole.

the thud

a sound, distant.
its weight presses the floorboards,
brimming in the glass of tea,
settling into the lines
of a paused hand, mid-air.

it stays outside the perimeter words.
its edges fray speech,
and the filaments of broken words
settle into the corners,
too small to name.

the thud carries the room,
its weight shifts the hour.

we cannot meet it.
our language slips.
all precision dissolves,
while the chairs, the window,
the air itself, lean toward it.

the sound frames the room,
holding its shape.

our words, a hollow echo,
speak of anything else.
and yet, it holds us,
its silence gathering around us.

sixth hour

*the sixth hour arrives at noon, when heat bears down and
shadows shorten.*

*these poems hold trial and sorrow, the silence of absence,
and the stark truth of mortality.*

*they face the cross by naming what is heavy and enduring the
press of its fire.*

*the reader is invited to enter this hour with courage, to carry
the weight of noon as a form of prayer.*

this little bird

this little bird waited for me,
its feathers dark with a shifting blue,
a single brightness in the bare tree,
still as a question that does not move.

its gaze held the air in place,
without stir or flutter.
my step slowed,
the silence gathered around us.

it offered nothing but presence,
yet the road changed as I passed,
and what was heavy within me
softened, lighter for a time.

the sway

roots prise open seams of rock,
iron rises sharp after rain,
leaves collapse into pulp.

air snaps in the pine crowns,
grit stings the mouth,
a bell strikes once,
the nave holds the silence.

clay splits in the kiln,
bronze pours to its mold,
bread opens along the cut,
embers glow against the wall.

a stream cuts through clay,
herons keep their stillness,
the moon shatters on its surface,
water closes smooth.

earth steadies the morning,
air carries the noon,
fire marks the evening,
water carries the night.
in their rhythm we rise and rest,
in their turning we are turned.

permanency and the snow

the ice lays its hand on the earth,
cold and still after the freeze.
we scrape against what resists,
tendons raw,
a fleeting victory
before the frost returns.

snow does not sweep itself away.
paths whiten again overnight,
layer upon layer,
a weight carried through seasons,
indifferent to our labor.
hoarfrost stings my face,
tears blur the shape of work,
the sun too thin to break its grip.

yet the thaw comes,
quiet, patient,
a soft drip loosening the edges.
we write our names in snow and wind,
knowing they will vanish,
yet leaving a trace in the act itself.

impermanence holds its own permanence.
each word that melts
returns in another form,
like a faint print pressed into ice,
waiting for light to uncover it again.

cataclysm

the water rained in from the window wells
just like that,
drop by drop
the whole wall was wept away from its foundation.

silt gave way to silence,
wood fed the worms.
this house leaned into ruin.
in the bowing archway,
i watched it fall.

the ant

i watch the ant
circle in on its own scent,
spiraling across the slope.
its path crosses itself,
then veers,
then closes again,
a geometry without exit.

i too have turned in such patterns,
believing each step new,
each curve a departure,
until the ground revealed
the same figure drawn again.

the ant keeps moving,
faithful to its turning,
carrying nothing but the circle,
endless, exact,
engraved into the day.

anche io

the centuries pass,
anche io passo, climbing the hill
where milkweed opens to monarch wings,
and stones lie patient in the grass.

i was a boy at noon,
a cenotaph by night.
tomorrow i will be ruin,
then silence, then dust.
each form a name
given back to the earth.

corpus manifesto

pain became number,
a measure of hours and wounds.
five struck, thirty paid,
twelve who fled,
three who slept.

at the sixth, the sky darkened,
at the ninth, the cry rose.
the tally was taken,
a sum written into flesh.

stones counted, dice cast,
garments split at the foot of the cross,
vinegar lifted on a reed,
a spear opening the side.
nothing escaped the ledger.

yet when the veil was torn,
the count fell silent.
the tomb sealed in stone
held no reckoning,
only emptiness opening,
where number dissolved into light.

thirty pieces

i counted the silver once,
its shine caught in the lines of my hand.
i spent it quickly,
and still the clink rang louder
than prayer in the night.

what i bought was ash,
what i kept was silence.
bread broken became stone,
and the cup would not lift.

betrayal walked beside me,
its shadow longer than mine.
it spoke with my voice,
and left me hollow
where trust had lived.

if truth remains,
let it be a stone unshattered,
let it be the coin i could not spend,
buried in the field
where blood darkens the soil.

feel of blood

soft is the flowing of blood,
quick the piercing of flesh,
a moment sharp and irretrievable,
more painful than the body admits.

soldiers smashed and sliced,
clubbed and cut through the sinews of strangers.
i recoil from their carnage,
the sight an error in the order of things.

blood clings thick and sweet,
a liquor of essence.
once it covered my hand,
warm and viscous,
as i helped a woman
in the moment after the cutting.

i wiped it on the grass,
blade against blade,
tracing lines into the earth,
my fingers catching on cracks.
the blood dried and my skin stiffened.
the sky broke open as she ran.
i ran too,
to wash my hands with soap and scalding water.

the feel lingers,
like a memory in the folds of skin,
never wholly washed away.

in the palaces

the first is still.
polished boards where moonlight slips,
a stain darkening the far corner,
oil or blood.
no one speaks of it.
the air carries iron,
sharp and metallic.

the second drones softly,
a sound caught in the walls,
threaded through the beams.
a lullaby,
a voice near and far,
its song unfinished, falling away.

in the third, moss climbs,
green spreading through the cracks.
the air smells of wet stone,
earth heavy with memory.
the ground shifts underfoot,
slow, deliberate.

the last palace waits.
the rooms still hold their heat,
thick in the air.
the ceiling leans low,
shadows pressing close.
you reach for a word,
but the silence rises,
and nothing follows.

when light came

when light came in the morning,
i broke too.

mountains stood.
they did not move.
it should be the soul
that shakes.

the pond showed the sky
on its surface.
stones lay beneath,
silent,
unshaken.

rich with autumn leaves,
i empty my hands,
poor in spirit.

begin with love,
or with hope,
at morning.

the river we remember swirls

still waters swirl and rage,
and i too rage,
sitting by the water's edge,
the wind waves the sea,
which splashes, unwelcome, on my face.

as i draw inside my firmament,
i rhyme of the stoics with all my shaking,
their columns standing solid in storms,
their wisdom the lead i attempt to follow.
my palms press to the ground,
seeking a rhythm older than the sea,
the weight of earth steady beneath me.

the waves shift, churning their own stories,
a hymn of motion without pause.
i listen as the tide stretches forward,
its reach brushing the shore,
its pull a quiet invitation.
this is the space i have sought,
a threshold where waiting begins,
where the water and the wind
offer no answers, only movement.

the wind brings voices
threaded through the air,
their syllables weaving paths toward me,
their call resonant and full.
i hear them without meaning,
a sound that rests in my chest,
a question asked in every wave.

i stand and step forward,
the water cool,
the sand soft beneath each footfall.
each moment oscillates with effort,
the tide pressing,
the far line unfastened.
there is no path,
only the shape of my own stride,
the rhythm of steps into the shallows.

the river rises,
its currents wrap around my legs,
a weight and a lift all at once.
i move deeper,
toward the voices,
toward the horizon,
each step a meeting,
each wave a passage.

the storm becomes a story
i carry within,
its rhythm the beat of motion,
its pull the echo of leaving
and arriving,
a call that carries onward.

he ran

he ran so hard, so fast,
for so long,
that the weight of his own lives
settled in his back and knees.

worries, regrets,
stacked and carried,
a history worn thin,
fractured into other names
he tried on
and left behind.

small injuries gathered,
layered without healing.
wound over wound,
some shallow,
some burrowed deep,
already changing beneath the skin.

the body was an adding machine.
each step heavier,
each imagining more borrowed
than the last.

no one saw the running.
only the slowing,
the stop.

adamantine

there was this faith,
and it was adamantine,
though even adamantium chips in time.

the erosion can be calculated.
real years traced in arcs around ourselves,
multiplied by fissures born each winter
and revealed each spring
by the freezing and thawing of our hearts.
all this, held in parentheses,
over our expectations.

then consumed,
like any dwelling in a dense, dry forest
when thunder growls and lightning smirks.
i am here,
curling inward after the conflagration,
where blood ignites,
burning along worn edges.
white-blue flames dissolve to grey,
ash settling in silence,
where skin cracks and yields
to the stillness that remains.

skotos

and so what
when i die.
today or tomorrow
is the same.
a name carved shallow
on limestone
washed by the deep.

i will walk like a mummy
in silver shoes
and silk robes
now frayed,
now feeding on insects,
and coins, left by the merciful,
through corridors
already claimed by the skotos,
dragging dust of forgotten processions.

if i were given forever
i would spend it
among broken amphorae
and the scent of damp stone.
if i were given a single hour
it might be enough
to remember the silence
of white-tiled halls.
too late, and too early in the day.

so what, then, today.
so what if tomorrow.
so what of my death
on all the other days
swallowed by a blank page.

down the creek
a leaf rests thin in the shallows,
its veins fine as script on worn parchment,
a page opened by water and light,
a testament no hand has inscribed.

stones gleam beneath the current,
their colors lifted into motion.
grasses press against the flow,
insects drift where brightness settles.

the surface weaves brightness and shadow,
a lattice shifting with each pulse,
a window cut through water and time,
a pattern drawn, withdrawn, renewed.

i linger where the creek recites itself,
a cadence older than memory,
its current steady as the turning hours,
its silence complete in its passage.

still it flows

there is a river
older than me,
older than you,
wider than kingdoms,
lower than the hush after prayer.

it runs through the broken heart of the world,
through the cracked bones of cities,
through the dust where names sleep.

it carries banners of mercy,
it bears victories of the unseen.
it moves with tenderness that endures.

those who kneel to drink from it
taste the ancient sweetness of life,
that strength which rises through sorrow.

this river flows through every hand lifted in thirst,
this river begins in the heart of mercy,
this river carries all who surrender to its current.

i have fallen into it,
still, it flows.

the sea vast

this is the sea, vast as forgetting,
its surface writing fleeting scriptures,
its depths, an atlas of the unseen,
whispering of what is held and never told.

beneath, shadows drift without witness,
fins cut through muted green,
shells collapse, bones settle,
a rhythm older than any name.

the tide hammers stone to powder,
pulls sand from under the step,
each surge erases the mark,
each return lays down new weight.

stars scatter on the black surface,
their light splintered into shards,
the moon fractures across the ripples,
then sinks into silence.

the sea holds no memory,
yet its floor is written with wrecks,
with anchors and timbers,
with the weight of all that has fallen in.

to stand here is to be measured,
to feel the scale of forgetting,
to know the body is small,
and the water unending.

the sadducee's shrug

there is no resurrection,
only repetition.
the sun returns,
but not the dead.

dust is only dust,
it does not remember
through personification.
the life that left our lungs
does not come back.

we sat near the temple,
watching the pilgrims
count their sins
in coins.

i asked
what rises
when the body fails.
they offered only a shrug.
the kind that flattens
parables into policy,
prophets into property.

if the soul is weightless, they said,
why does it take
so many laws
to lift?

and when the man rose,
they cleared their throats,
adjusted their robes,
and called it
a metaphor.

the vines

what will i do with the sadness
through these long orange days,
my head bent inward,
my arms lost to the night.

fear grows like vines,
twisting through the labyrinth
of thought, coiling tighter
around the softest places.

here is my pulse,
shallow and borrowed,
and my heartbeat, fragile,
held out to the quiet.

the vines climb higher,
reaching toward the light
or some imagined escape.
what blade could free me.

the day burns, its flame low,
its edges curling into ash.
the night presses heavy,
its weight a question i cannot lift.

i wait for the clearing,
for a crack in the shadow,
for the vines to fall away,
or bloom into something whole.

pretty lies

look at all the pretty lies.
how they took from me my little time,
what small time I had to hold.

there is the void,
the place where time slips through,
always too little,
always too late.

all the pretty lies,
with their many textures and colours,
shimmer for a moment in the marketplace,
then fade to dust.
but they are the dust,
glittering just long enough
to blind the eyes,
their beauty made of wobbly mirrors
and bending light.

and now,
as they scatter to corners
I had thought were empty,
I sit among their remnants,
feeling the weight of silence,
the weight of what I cannot hold.

this is the inheritance of light.
it shines for a moment,
then folds itself into shadows.

the last

i am the last of me.
will you renew me,
you who held my name.

my years have bloomed,
petals dewed with time,
into minutes drawn long,
ripe and unfinished.

the final gasp waits,
full of teeth and bone,
an appetite rising,
drawn to the rim of the cup,
where holy water warms
against the lip.

renew some faith in me.
for i have run in the same circle
as wild men and klephts,
my steps firm
against the stone of the world.

i matched their pace
when the path was clear,
named each wind
by what it took from me.

i carried fire,
though it burned through the cloth.
i drank the dark water
and howled when it passed.

you saw me stand.
you saw me stay.

once again and again

counsel calls,
threaded through the fabric of hours,
present in each word spoken,
in the spaces where thought rests,
waiting for us to attend,
waiting for us to enter.

we rise each day,
offering ourselves to the current
that carries us through time.
each stride is devotion,
each thought a renewal,
a turning back to what the body already knows,
to the truth that moves with us
through shadow and brightness,
through what we carry and release.

the day itself becomes offering,
spoken without sound.
we walk forward,
open to counsel that shows us what is near
yet still unseen.
each moment is an opening,
each passage draws us deeper into truth.

as evening lowers,
we pause,
yet the search continues.
it moves between waking and sleep,
in the hush that gathers around us,
in the places where peace settles.
again we lean toward prayer,
again toward attending,
again toward yielding.

understanding moves unseen,
a current through all things.
we receive what is given,
we enter what has always been here.

we are carried by the search,
shaped by the offerings we make.
we walk in it,
stride by stride,
letting each moment unfold.
truth abides in attending,
in the readiness to yield
to what is present.

we lose ourselves,
yet the way remains steady,
drawing us forward
with the pulse beneath each stride.
devotion carries us toward what cannot be grasped
but can be received.
we move, guided by what is unseen,
guided by what stands before us,
awaiting discovery.

each psalm circles back,
each stride renews us
in the world where counsel abides.
we rise once more,
entering the rhythm
that endures.

the search continues,
seeking the ground that bears truth,
the place where understanding speaks.
we pass through day and night,
through silence that teaches,
through presence that speaks without words.

each day is an offering,
each stride an offering,
each prayer a movement forward
into what has always been near.
there is only the entering,
the attending,
the receiving.

we go on,
one movement at a time,
trusting the current
that threads through all things,
trusting the counsel that leads us deeper
into mystery.

in seeking we are filled,
in searching we are shaped.
wisdom draws us closer,
always here,
always present.
we step forward once more,
and in the return we find truth
that has always been here,
waiting for us to attend,
waiting for us to open.

ninth hour

the ninth hour bends toward grief and mercy.

the poems in this section acknowledge loss, yet they also find fidelity within it.

this is the hour when memory deepens and endurance steadies the heart.

the reader is invited to enter this hour with honesty, letting memory and lament shape a way into mercy.

the one who stays

a hush with wings
from the milkweed field
to the moss-soft shore.
she walked with me,
stride for stride,
sharing the weight of my shadow.

she shimmered like wind-caught silk,
laughter pooled
in the stream's throat.

from the slow funicular,
i saw her below,
dancing
in the orange flowers and wild grass, watching.

an ember in daylight in the olive air,
she followed where the trail bent
toward the sorrow-hill,
her warmth the hour's only language.

when the hill bloomed sorrow,
and no voice rose,
she stayed.

the horizon gives way

the sky leans forward where it meets the ocean,
a line drawn soft by light and distance.
each wave arrives with what will not be named,
a rhythm older than voices, still carried.

the water glitters, full of more than joy.
it stretches from the stone edge to the farthest shimmer,
and lifts toward the sun with ease,
offering only motion, and the depth of shimmer.

between my eyes and the long blue seam of horizon,
a group of men lie back in the sand.
their shoulders gleam with oil and late-day heat,
and their laughter rises like gulls above the brine.

their presence brings back the hush of a field,
a face half-turned in the tall grass.

my skin recalls the taste before it reaches my tongue.
i walked from the high path toward the water below,
past olive trees and the hush of painted icons,
past monks who moved as if walking through prayer.

the tide marked what it would carry,
quiet in its rhythm, slow in its claim.
i felt the pull before i understood its name.

here is my pain, in the slant of light across wet stone,
held in the curve of a swimmer's back,
folded into a child's abandoned sandals,
pressed into sand that waits for the water to return.

i sit and watch, carried by the quiet.
the ocean moves, steady in its rhythm.
the sky opens again, pale with evening.
the horizon gives way, and nothing is separate.

wax and parchment

this love is wax and parchment,
steeped in dark tea moons,
stamped with a gold ring
that rose from the source
of our thirst.

these are words.
gold is gold.
your eyes: dusk and thirst.

lift me up,
as you did when the sky split,
cranking this hand-braided rope,
though my waters are murky,
my scent leaf and copper.

i am thirsty for the bright of day,
for the cracks where it bleeds in.
i am thirsty for your lips,
their parched geography,
their salt.

unmoving

i have scavenged for my sanity
like the squirrels in early spring,
those same squirrels who return
to the soil they marked in autumn.

i imagine them certain,
claws landing within an inch
of what was hidden.

they scatter as i pass,
but something in their movement
draws me closer,
a reminder.

i once buried my mind with care,
held it through frost,
through hibernation,
through ice.

the spring returns.
it always does,
whether we rise to meet it
or lie beneath it,
unmoving.

the relic

i loved you genuinely.
so i'll avoid arguments over words.

we know what love is.
love is the flame,
not the ashes left behind.
like marble blistered by persian fires,
i am hunched and scorched,
encased in glass,
displayed in an istanbul museum.

i loved you like the skin remembers the burn.
like cement poured to protect what poisons.
this love.
sadness cupped in the palm of my hand,
a relic too fragile to hold.
a tragedy tucked inside something ordinary.

there are depths of solitude

there are depths of solitude
washed in pastel watercolour,
in the fullness of your cheek,
in branches bare of leaves,
in long shadows
mid-november, in these parts.

it has snowed,
or its coming is felt as cold air rising
from somewhere deeper than despair,
pulling longing with it.

you are accompanied by the moon tonight,
steady above the thinning trees.
what offers a finer backdrop
than this harvest light.

you wear it
as if it were glass, fused and cool,
casting the night
against your unspoken thoughts.

when light waits

the light had not stolen into the room,
ducking behind blackout curtains
we hung years ago,
hoping for mornings
when the world could wait.
but it rarely does.

morning slept.
i was awake again,
waking without wanting to wake,
the reticence pressing against me
like the weight of unopened eyes.
i watched shadows shift,
soft edges creeping
as the hours grew long.

waiting for others to stir,
for life to resume its quiet commotion,
i lay still,
not wanting to shatter the quiet,
even as it crept into my chest,
a slow, familiar ache.
the light outside, patient as death,
waited too.

time bends differently here.
these hours between dreaming and waking.
curtains hold back the sun,
but not the gentle pull of day,
drawing me out,
pressing me into its rhythm,
where the light no longer waits.

echo of heat

blistered and raw, heat rises in waves,
skin lit like embers beneath a touch,
flushed with the echo of heat.

balm slicks the burn, slow and shining,
a second skin spread by careful hands,
coating what glows, what refuses to cool.

thought catches flame,
the mind sparks like scorched metal,
glowworm red, remembering fire,
oil clinging thick on the skin.

days leave their mark pressed deep,
a covering impossible to wash away.

the body learns to bear its own heat,
to carry the burn, to shine beneath it,
to slip through the world slick with sorrow,
cool to the touch, yet burning beneath,
untouched, untouched, never unmarked,
marked by the glisten of the burn.

tulips in bloom

do you know if the tulips are in bloom.
i saw them creeping last month,
pushing through the muddy cold,
their green spears cautious,
hesitant to commit.

now it is wet and warm,
and grass fuzz gathers
in the bare patches
near the lavender tree,
a tree planted
beside the electrical box,
that green obelisk,
made invisible
by the insistence of its being,
always there, always ignored.

like the tulips,
which wait in the ground one day
and the next,
their ruby-red petals
are swept into the grass,
a burst colour.

so soon risen,
so soon in bloom,
so soon to spill their life
back into the earth,
like osiris,
whose name we speak softly,
as though it holds
the memory of permanence.

he is buried in the back of the yard,
beneath the mulberry tree,
where the earth stays damp,
where the grass refuses
to grow too thick.

the tulips remind me of him.
a life that rises,
blooms fiercely,
and falls,
its brilliance returning
to the soil,
feeding what comes next.

do you know if the tulips are in bloom.
perhaps they are osiris
reaching up again,
each spring a fleeting gesture,
a brief hymn sung
to the cycle that carries us all.

texture of light

fright is a feeling,
and it carries degrees.

terror waits at one end.
a boy i knew in school stands at the other,
his highest ambition to tip cows
on dark roads where no one watched.

light also refuses measure.
it is wave and particle.
it slips from the box
and will not stay
while we press it against our designs.

once, a band of light crossed the closet door.
mauve traced its edge,
colors rare and unfamiliar.

it seemed drawn by a hand
steady enough to carve stone,
too fine, too exact
to come by accident.

the door was painted taupe.
the light impossibly clean.
i stood there,
uncertain if this was paint
or reflection,
a single perfect line
thrown across the room by some chance
that placed me where it fell.

it startled me, the way light sometimes startles.

i reached out,
confused by what my eyes offered.

my hand found air.
the light held nothing
my skin could feel.

shape

a wet shirt clings to the spine,
sags the sheet,
until the sleep
pools into your hip bone.

ash gathers at the base of the neck.
the sheet is twisted, or it is me twisting,
cool in one place,
duress in another.

i heard the birds as if they were motorbikes,
hearkening a day of commotion in the street,
rather than the stillness that followed.

morning is not arrival.
it is the end of holding still.

love too vast for silence

i name you never, for names are parapets,
and love as deep as this
swallows the surface of words,
subsuming the world's thin lines,
a tide rising without call.

if i could still my mind, i would,
but you have made it a lantern,
cut open like a diorama,
each thought a window where light
escapes in quiet rivers,
gold pooling at my feet like something sacred.

i would say nothing,
for silence is fair,
but love this vast refuses rest,
it runs through marrow,
unraveling the hush i try to keep.

i would crumble into eggshells,
but you,
you are the soft weight of dusk upon my shoulders,
the sky learning patience before the stars arrive,
the tide knowing when to rest upon the shore.

inheritance

i take what's given,
fingers closing before thought,
the weight less than expected,
until it isn't.

i am the one carrying work,
bone hollowed by its crawl,
sleep entering with a clenched hand,
a shoulder pulled from warmth.

i am the one watching,
time thinning in the doorway,
the road empty until it ends,
the silence of rooms
heavier than speech.

i am the one counting,
palms cracked, my mouth tasting of metal,
days stacked like coins,
nights like ash,
wondering how loss could pass as gift.

i am the one hungering,
feet bruised with distance,
spine bracing with its ache,
mouth full of unswallowed words,
harsh, too sharp to swallow.

i am the one remembering,
a table laid before hunger spoke,
plates cold to the touch,
a ring dulled from waiting,
bread unbroken,
a place set for absence.

i am the one returning,
standing where the road ends,
where the house begins,
holding what will not fit
in the hollow of the mouth.

and i am the one lurching,
without choosing toward or away,
into the emptiness that remains,
full of the weight of names,
full of what follows.

this is how we go

there is no before.
no after stretches from now.
chests rise, falling.
each blink is a coffee spoon
measuring out our mornings.

we move because we wind down,
keys turned tight, springs ticking,
arms swinging with nowhere to land,
legs marching to no command,
moments slipping loose
while the day tilts forward.

time vanishes whenever it pleases,
slipping into rhyme,
minutes dissolving between hiccups and snorts,
days pressing into each other,
edges blurred beyond recall.

this is how we go.
blinks into hours,
twitches into days,
measured out and spent.

rooted stillness

frost lay across the field,
each stalk brittle under my step.
my exhalation ghostly white,
lifting and breaking in the morning cold.

the well kept open,
its rim rough with lichen,
stone damp where the frost had melted.
below, the water shifted faintly,
a dark circle unfreezing,
its surface gathering small rings
from something unseen.

i listened for the echo,
leaned over the stone lip,
let my voice fall.
it struck the depth and returned thin,
a sound stretched by distance,
wavering in the cool air.

the ground above was stiffening,
streams already narrowed with ice,
but here the water turned inward,
quiet, deep, unbroken.

i stood with my hands on the stone,
the morning held still around me.
the water moved beneath,
its dark turning steady,
the sound of depth waiting
as the cold pressed harder,
and for a moment, light gathered in the dark.

crossing

in the quiet where thought dissolves,
a stillness opens, vast and unbound,
a bridge begins, unseen at first,
its lines delicate as a string drawn taut,
its rhythm unfolding, motion by motion.

beneath, the tide scatters and reforms,
a fleeting world of currents undone.
its echoes brush the edges of this depth,
while inward, a silence endures,
untouched by the ceaseless turning.

here, time is infinite and slow,
a moment held, expanding and whole.
each step shaping what is to come,
each stride unravels what came before.
light falls through branches that hold no name,
questions unspoken linger in its wake.

this is the crossing, the unmapped place,
where what is seen slips into what is felt.
both are pain, each is redemptive,
their meeting a chord struck, clear and sweet.

the bridge stretches, endless and fleeting,
its pull unknown until the passage is made.
a quiet drift through a widening sky,
its horizons folding outward, unbound.
here, the self is iteratively transformed yet steady,
its shape released, then made whole again.

at the far end, the bridge dissolves,
folding into air, infinite and unbound.
the self stands unknowing and renewed,
its voice lifted,
a hymn to what waits beyond.

days of creation

beneath warmth, beneath rivered ramparts,
they rise and fall,
kingdoms waking in the stir of hunger,
nations fading in the hush of rest.

they toil where sight cannot reach,
shaping what sustains the whole,
passing labours hand to hand,
tides unseen before the hour turns auburn.

one effort, the next,
what falls away will rise again,
folded into the hunger of need.

the body follows the turn of fields,
the shift of air along its skin,
what was brittle greens again,
what was tender readies and tightens.

a city lifts its walls,
a child stretches farther than before,
a hand finds stone to carve,
in time, the stone smooths,
the city folds into dust,
the child becomes the builder.

what was given is given again,
woven into the turning.

a hundred winters press my limbs,
soft in the hush of slow growth,
rings deepen where years have gathered,
each pressed by the earth's slow shift.

the rivers call as they did before men,
before the cut of road, before the rise of iron,
they have turned to time's pull,
but i remain, keeping the hush of centuries.

what changes in the span of a leaf,
a city raised and emptied,
a tongue carried to silence,
the bones of those who shaped the earth.

a single light breaks across the dark,
born from fire that burned before empires,
the pulsation of stars scatters dust into orbits,
throws them into turning.

a redwood stands in its quiet age,
an elder reaches for something unseen,
a kingdom vanishes, its stones scattered,
while the sky holds its old fires.

all move within the hush of my arms,
woven into the course of what has been,
and what will be.

each to its rhythm,
each within the great motion.

hands build and pass,
fields ready and rest,
trees hold the patience of time,
sky carries all it has given.

all within the whole,
all carried forward,
creation moves through all things,
folding what was into what will be,
again, and again, and again.

while the world unravels

you stood in the eye of a hurricane,
poised in its rainless hollow,
your silhouette carved against a world unraveling.
the wind lifted an alligator from the water,
its body twisting like a creature unmoored from dreams.
it hovered mid-air,
eyes wide with bewilderment,
and waved,
a strange, almost tender gesture,
as if acknowledging its role in this tableau.
then it vanished,
swallowed by the storm's whirling maw.

you were still,
unshaken,
the air circumnavigating your calm.
your voice rose steady, deliberate,
charting the storm's trajectory,
while your knees rested lightly on a turkey wing,
and steam from cider curled in your hands.
it could have been a prayer,
that moment,
where the ordinary met the sublime,
and chaos bowed to ritual.

behind you, the storm churned,
indifferent to the weight of your stillness.
trees broke like brittle bones,
waters roared and claimed the earth,
yet you remained,
a quiet center in the hurricane's hymn,
a figure caught between absurdity and grace.

was it courage,
to sip cider while the world fell apart?
or simply the art of living,
of finding thanksgiving
in the small, the fleeting,
the warmth of cider,
the humour of a waving alligator,
the knowledge that storms, too, must pass?

and so we watched you,
entranced by your quiet defiance,
your presence a strange and perfect beauty,
a reminder that even in chaos,
there is room for stillness.
and when the storm moves on,
as storms always do,
we will remember you standing there,
inactive,
a silhouette against the shifting winds,
your cider cooling,
your voice steady as the turning earth.

sycamore

i climb my sycamore,
the tree of my youth,
the one that held me
before i knew the weight of being seen.

the tools wait below,
their handles worn smooth,
each groove pressed with years of work.
the voices rise from the crowd,
a wave breaking beneath me,
their faces blurred, their hands restless.

the tree stands as it always has,
its limbs reaching beyond the noise,
a ladder to the air above.

each step draws me upward,
each branch steady beneath my grasp.
the city sharpens below,
its streets and rooftops
laid bare as patterns i had once forgotten.

here i am, zacchaeus,
awkward, exposed,
held by this tree
that knows my years.
the years i stole,
the years i gave away.
i am old and young,
me, reborn as me.

i climb despite the crowd,
i fill out the space above them,
where the light gathers,
where i might finally see
how goodness wears its robes.

the descent is slower,
each step pressing me closer
to the ground that waits.
the bark leaves its mark on my hands,
its lines mapping the path i have taken.

the tools wait where they always have,
their edges ready,
their balance unchanged,
but my hands are steadier.

the sycamore stands,
its roots deep,
its branches wide as an offering.
the world below is the same,
but i have seen and been seen,
and i carry less than when i climbed.

short in stature,
how might i still see.
between words

talking past one another
feels like frost crawling across still water,
its lines spreading without sound,
holding no warmth, only distance.
we leave the words behind,
dinner plans, work days,
the heaviness pressing near my eye,
and the faint scent of philosophy
caught in the fold of the new yorker.

snow leans heavily into the windows,
its weight soft and insistent.
light spills from the farthest room,
a dim pulse stretching thin.

hibernation begins with small gestures,
the book resting unopened on the table,
a hand paused too long on the back of a chair.
steam rises from the kettle,

spiraling into the dim air.
outside, frost laces its threads
over trees stripped bare.

your voice once moved through this house
like the lake in its summer fullness,
wide and sure, rippling with its own life.
now it presses faintly, a crack beneath ice,
a memory folding inward, buried in cold water.
i lean into the silence,
but it offers nothing in return.

the hours fold into themselves.
books press close on the shelf,
their pages untouched,
their weight thick in waiting.
a clock ticks faintly,
its rhythm folding time into the dimness.
the fire shrinks low in its corner,
its whispers trailing into the night.
beyond the windows, winter presses near.

beneath the frost, water begins to stir.
the lake laps softly,
its voice curling through the frozen layers.
a shoe rests crooked by the stair,
its partner half-forgotten near the door.
snow drapes over bare branches,
each flake adding its quiet weight.

beneath the ice, the lake holds its weight,
water pressed into silence,
roots sprawling in the unseen dark.
the frozen surface gleams faintly,
like glass that once carried heat.
everything here sharpens.
the shadows press deeper,
edges pull closer to their source.

your letters rest beneath the day's paper,
holding the cedar's ghost in their folds.
your hand remains in the crease,
its weight as familiar as your voice once was.
i imagine the words pressed tightly inside,
curled like roots in winter,
and leave them unopened,
their silence enough.

you said silence was its own weather,
a season that asks us to wear it fully.
it fills the house like a coat meant for the cold,
thick, heavy, lasting through endless nights.
the air settles firmly against the walls,
carrying its own kind of certainty,
its presence motionless, undeniable.

the thaw begins without ceremony,
a slow loosening beneath the surface.
the lake murmurs as the ice shifts,
its voice low and deliberate,
its ripples stretching faintly.
the moon slides through a line of trees,
its light spilling softly over snow,
and somewhere, a branch begins to crack free.

the lake exhales its silence.
ice releases, water swells,
each movement deliberate, sure,
returning to the rhythm of its depths.
frost lingers at the shore's edge,
but the water stretches outward,
catching the sun's slow hand,
its surface widening into light.

one cold day

we walked as far as the lake this morning,
your hand grazing mine as the wind rose.
the short bay lapped with ice,
clusters breaking apart, sloshing and pooling,
their sound stitched into our steps,
curling through the air like a thread pulled loose.
the water's motion felt unending,
its persistence pressing into the absence between us
as we moved toward the skyline.

at home, the books leaned
where we had left them, curved
like familiar shoulders.
the kettle bubbled to a beep,
its steam rising unevenly.
on the table, a copy of the new yorker lay,
its corners curling like the edges of the lake,
its pages marked by damp air
and the weight of my heavy hand.

your voice came gently then,
unrushed, softened by the morning light.
you spoke of the lake and how it never truly froze,
how even in winter it pressed against the shore.
your words drifted steady as tide against sand,
deliberate, each one brushing the frame of the room.
i traced the rim of my mug with my finger,
the rhythm familiar,
the sound of your voice blending with the fire.

our gas fire glowed quietly in the corner,
its flickering light steady and insistent.
we leaned into each other, shoulders touching,
our silence woven through the room.
outside, the branches stirred faintly,
their smallest twigs snagging in the breeze.

nothing in the world stood still.
everything, even the air itself,
leaned toward the invisible.

later, we opened a book together,
its spine cracked softly in your hands,
the pages opening into place.
you read aloud, stories of sea and shore,
words that moved with the hush of a tide.
i followed each line with my fingertip,
drawing a quiet map,
each word lapping softly at the edges of thought.

the afternoon deepened,
its light fading slowly as clouds gathered.
we walked again,
the gravel crunching underfoot,
your scarf trailing behind you,
the air pressing against us like an old friend.
the lake greeted us, restless as ever,
its ice smacking and splintering,
its margins crackling with sound.

we stood still at the shore,
watching the clusters of ice shift and collapse.
you pointed toward the far side of the lake,
to where the light spilled thin between clouds.
it stretched across the water
like the crease in a well-worn page,
its glow quiet but certain,
as though it had always been there.

evening spread around us,
its colors soft as brushed paper.
we walked home together,
the sound of the lake following us,
quiet and unrelenting,
its rhythm folding into our steps,
a reminder of something steady, something whole.

at home, the books leaned patiently,
their stories still waiting to be told.
the fire clicked softly as it dimmed,
its glow fading but not gone.
you rested your head against my shoulder,
and we let the day ease into the room,
its weight gentle, its warmth enduring,
its presence undeniable.

the lake drifted with us through the night.
its voice folded into our dreams,
its edges carried the memory of motion,
a quiet promise to hold,
to reach, again and again,
its rhythm as steady as love.
its predestined place

the glass tilts,
jarred by a fumbling hand,
shaky with excess living.
water slips in a thin stream.
it gathers in the grooves of the table,
darkening the wood in uneven lines.
ink spreads across the page,
a bloom unraveling slowly,
its edges uneven,
its movement deliberate.

strips of horizontal light stretch through the blinds,
drawing faint patterns on the surface of the table.
headlights sweep past,
their glow catching briefly on the plaster,
then fading in dissipation of light.

clicks from the clock,
rhythms steady,
uneven, measure
out the stillness as music.

hands hover above the notebook,
then pull back.
the wood beneath feels cool,
the ink's stain settling into permanence,
its edges drying
as water pools deeper into the grain.

the ink spreads like rain once pooled on a windowsill,
water tracing its rhythm on the glass.
the table recalls fingers pressing fast
into frayed pages,
the sound of a door closing,
heavy, final.

the ink halts the page,
its bloom complete.
the decision follows,
slipping into the grooves of the table,
settling like water,
finding its predestined place.

vespers

vespers gathers the day as it yields to evening.

the poems carry thanksgiving, gratitude for what endures, and acceptance of what fades.

this is the hour of closure, when dusk softens in colour and prayer rise in fullness.

the reader is invited to let the day settle into balance, offering what has been lived back to the source of life.

i have walked this city

the city moves fast.
i cannot match the lights,
red to green,
green to gone.
pause, and you might pass,
if you might,
if you dare
to dodge the motorbikes
and marble fragments,
jutting like bones.

i sleep above a string of lights,
strung like memory
over stone-laid lanes,
where webs of wandering tongues
catch me mid-sentence,
then slip.

a woman speaks,
her son responds,
both at once,
listening, speaking,
no silence between them.
making meaning
in the spaces i stumble through
and interrupt.

here is athena, raised on a column.
there, an owl
tessellated in the ancient floor.
another bust leans into the wall.
and the clerics,
they carry books like tools,
building belief
from broken belief,
same words,
new scaffolds.

yesterday i passed the temple of artemis
and wandered into a monk's graveyard,
tucked behind basilicas
and the feet of columns.

my skin flakes in the midsummer sun,
dust falling like the rain that seldom comes.
settling on the ancients like prayer ash.
i am older still.
i have walked this city,
and i will return
as dust.

florence again

the quarter opens with narrow stone corridors.
pavement curves without ornament.
surfaces meet at quiet angles.

steps lead through a city built for walking.
light arrives without display.
a chapel stands at the corner without announcement.
letters are carved into marble.

beatrice appears in narrow lines.
virgil rests beneath a roman arch.
dante is placed above the entrance
to a building once used for judgment,
still upright,
still open to the street.

i carry a book with blank pages.
each sheet waits for measure and phrase.
lines begin with rhythm,
formed slowly and without conclusion.
the page stays folded in my coat
as i walk along the route i traced before.

inside the chapel, the air rests in full shape.
columns support what rises above them.
light falls at deliberate angles.
stillness surrounds the figures who remain.
each stands without movement or sound.

i sang her song

i sang her song
in a language beyond my grasp,
a space untethered from rules
that once anchored me.

she moved with jagged grace,
bobbing in the wave,
her body bending to music
only she could hear,
a rhythm dissolving the tide.

my voice unspooled,
threading through her movement,
an interruption sharp enough
to fray her motion,
to scatter my serenity into sound.

for inspiration

all in one day,
i found peace. i hit the thing. i burned the wood.
i hated life, the shell of me.
all in one day,
i became the poem, the poetry, a thing of ruin,
or comedy a laugh like glass breaking.
i climbed then fell,
my skull hitting a metal sky,
its blue a razor, its black a leak,
its hate pressed into bone.

this sky broke my body,
sifting friendships into fine dust.
i age like a small creature moving fast,
each afternoon a smaller portion than the last,
each moment scraping closer to dirt
not soft powder, but crushed rock
broken by beginnings
too hard to forget.

the dark will come,
and i will crawl into it.
for now, i will sleep.
my days scattered in thought,
a quiet shock of words still vibrating from their first hit.

cyprian

you have a green zone.
i have a green zone.
both are splattered in blood.

green is the color of money
pressed into blood in iraq.
green is the eye of a monster
that mocks and feeds.

rage does not fade with age,
the rage of seeing what others will not see,
of speaking, unheard, inside athena's mist.

green is as old as venetians and moors.

have you walked a green line,
past empty storefronts,
broken windows,
a time machine coated in sadness.

silent, but if you turn the corner,
life moves at the edge
of the city's caldera,
burning brightest
where the line cuts green into earth and stone.

some cities carry that scar.
today, as every year,
dust piles high on barricades,
coils of wire
ensuring green will never return.

even the sun lowers its gaze
at how we divide ourselves
and the earth beneath us,
as if humanity and sand
could ever be torn apart.

alas for

alas for your ambition,
to be both bride and groom,
to hold the veil,
and lift it.

i am not constant as a clock,
nor fixed within any casing.
the hours pass,
and i am elsewhere.

my belt is leather,
worn smooth,
but never butter to the touch.
you would bruise your hands,
searching for softness.

alas, you wanted vows spoken,
and vows returned,
the circle closed by your own mouth.

i am not a mirror.
the ceremony cannot make me whole
within your hands.

do not trust me

the author begins here.
he writes what he writes,
and calls it true.
a reader turns the page,
words lie flat,
ink pressed into paper.

we are drawn toward knowledge

we are drawn
towards knowledge just as much
as we are repelled by it.
by its promise of arrival.
by the clean certainty of having known.

but we might be wise
to begin where sophocles ends.
oedipus, blinded by his own hands,
shows us that sight is not foresight.
we see, but not ahead.

and foresight is useless.
the paths we run, the turns we take,
whether direct or meandering,
lead us where the ground
was already set.

we dance,
believing the music is ours.
we fall,
thinking the stone was chance.

but the place was waiting.
the script already written.
sight or blindness changes nothing.

cosmopolitan

loneliness begins in the chest,
a hollow widening between heartbeats,
as stars widen their distance at night,
each pulse a planet held in silence.

the earth turns beneath us,
its oceans moving like blood in the body,
its forests rising, veins of deep green,
its clouds dispersing like thought.

if the earth can bear its solitude,
spinning with no answer but its orbit,
we too might root into stillness,
feet pressed to soil,
eyes open to the field of stars.

the body and the sky
both vessels of quiet fire,
carry the weight of continuance,
enduring as stone,
turning as the earth turns.

the halls are quiet

the corridor echoes with a single step.
papers curl at the edges of the notice board.
rows of chairs wait,
their silence deeper than voices.

a voice once steady has gone thin,
and the pause spreads through the room.
we hear it in slowed conversations,
in the way doors close softly,
as though guarding what is fragile.

students gather with notebooks open,
their eyes searching for what will hold.
faculty lean forward in their chairs,
hands folded, listening.
the work has not stopped,
but it turns, uncertain.

this is the moment
when the task moves to many hands.
not one voice, but a chorus,
layered and uneven,
stronger in its joining.

we speak of what endures:
questions written in margins,
a promise to listen,
a book passed from hand to hand.
we trust in the long labour of teaching,
a work that continues through us.

and still we say together:
this is the work.
this is the labour.
this is the light we keep.

no single hand will carry this.
we build the rhythm together,
day into night,
lesson into lesson.
the light is kept in the joining,
not in a star,
but in a lamp lifted,
so another may see to write.

and still we say together:
this is the work.
this is the labour.
this is the light we keep.

the train

i am the train,
hurtling through hours,
a needle stitching one life to another,
fraying at both ends.
the rhythm rocks me,
the sway belongs elsewhere,
never here, never now.

i count the absences:
a laugh lost at the platform,
a porch light flickering out,
faces i might have loved
left waiting in the smoke.

the miles fold into themselves
like thin paper in the hands of the creator
i fold into myself,
a plate of lead.
arrival comes heavy,
its silence greater than distance.
the train rocks on
while my chest holds still.
even the heart tires
of beating against steel.

i am the train,
but the hours claim me,
blurring until there are no edges,
only the relentless sway
of what i was meant to be.

days blur to wool and fog.
sleep stretches thin.
even my dreams fall quiet,
their voices gone unheard.
the train moves without stillness.
i sink into the rocking,

losing the measure of myself.

the thread tightens,
a hold against the sway.
the rhythm softens,
its grip loosens.

steel gives way to memory.
the track no longer endless.
i see the distance,
but it does not bind me.
i feel the pull of ground,
something steady,
a place i can name.

i wake to the chorus of light,
to windows opening,
to voices that rise together.
the train comes still.
i step forward.
i am here.
the hours are mine to hold.

rolling hills

you are my regent of these rolling hills,
the ones we pass on bumpy trains,
and suzerain of these waters,
still in the hollows, falling from ledges,
fresh as fruit, bronzed as earth.
over the animals pressed in foliage,
you are lord, and of the foliage too,
needles sharp against air and skin.

bring me all things,
the finest and those unnamed.
bring yourselves bent at waist and neck,
to take a gift.
i am benefaction,
liquid light pouring into valleys.
this land runs far,
it holds the sun in its rising,
it holds the words spoken in that light.

i hold music that moves off your rhythm.
i hold fire that thins in the night.
midas takes my crown.
prometheus grips my hands.
the age of gold falls into ash.
the age of fire passes hand to hand,
each flame heavier than the last.

the rolling hills remain,
the waters fall,
the animals burrow in roots,
and you stay,
king of all,
a silence turning in my hands.

beyond the hills,
rivers run with dust and stone,
temples rise of flesh and bone,
their blessings hard and hidden.

the sun lifts over the hills,
light pools in the folds of earth.
roots take water,
branches bend to it.
the valley opens,
the fields green,
the air bright with its own measure.

see and snow

where do you go,
once i can no longer see you,
once you pass the edge,
the sun trailing your steps into haze.

where do you go,
heels striking patches of ice,
each step cracking a brittle silence,
brave as aesop's lions,
anger faint under frost,
wind carving rivers into your face.

where have you gone,
beyond the reach of my hands,
past the fold of my voice.
you leave me shaping small worlds,
their lines aligned like pressed leaves.
each curve blooms into tulips,
petals exact,
offering something both brief and enduring.

where are you now,
when you could sit beside me,
our bodies bent like rowers in a trireme,
elbows raw, feet blistered from long wars.
let us throw our shoulders into the rhythm,
find strength in shared weight.

where have you gone,
and what have you seen
in the hours i cannot follow.
the snow gleams across the field,
its surface whole, its skin of light.
the sea lifts its silver tide,
waves folding into waves,
their rhythm unbroken.
your way moves there,
in snow that shines,
in water that keeps its motion,
quiet, certain, enduring.

name my moon

to name you my moon
would presume me a planet,
a force steady, orbit-worthy,
and that feels wrong.
planets carry weight,
but what i hold feels lighter,
less like pulling
and more like drifting into your tides.

you shimmer without anchor,
luminous in a way
that rises even when the sky
turns its face.
there is no borrowed, reflected light,
only the slow fire of your quiet burning,
a glow spilling over,
touching all that leans toward you.

to call you mine
would bind what moves freely.
your rhythm carries oceans,
softening even the most distant shores.
to name you my moon
would make me the center,
but all i feel is the spinning,
the falling toward you,
a dance that unspools gravity itself,
unclaimed, unnamed.

you are
the shimmer on a crest.
the planet, the orbit,
the pull and the letting go.
everything moves within you,
and i,
an oblate
in your endless glow.

the wheel

let us turn the wheel,
its rim slick with dawn,
iron smelling of rain,
rust staining the hands that hold it.

it carries straw caught in the spokes,
a feather from a sparrow's wing,
a pebble lodged tight against the hub,
the road's loose offerings.

pushed once, it rolls uneven,
a lurch over gravel,
a thud where the earth dips,
a screech when it gathers speed.

children chase it downhill,
their shouts skipping ahead,
bare feet slapping wet mud,
palms reaching for its spin.

by evening it rests against the fence,
paint chipped, rim leaning into grass,
ants crawling the grooves,
dew gathering again.

morning's balance

one eye opens, a thread of light,
a body unravels from the dark of night.
one foot steps to a magic rug,
the other to the bare, stark floor.
the day begins bright and chill, the air aglow.
steps whiten, laced with traces left,
and the promise of more snow.

snow will come as it must, as it dreams,
formed in quiet beyond what is seen.
its making a mystery, tender and still,
woven by wind, shaped by will.
no sound to its fall, no weight in its glide,
snow gathers as the sky's own tide.
and i, between what bends and stays,
rise to meet the lighted haze.
thin as frost, fierce as fire.

joy appears where snowflakes fall,
covering hollows, touching all.
a gale's embrace, the world enclosed,
pillowed nests and seams composed.
as snow drifts high, we drift below,
carried by currents we cannot know.
this morning holds us, whole, alive,
a trembling hush, the morning alive.

squared light

it waits, compact as a secret,
carried in the mass of a moment,
potential pressed into stillness,
held tightly in what exists.
love is dynamite,
fire stored in silence,
a french press, half full, growing warm.

when it ignites, it consumes,
radiates with the strength of stars,
splits the sky open
with its sudden force.
it spreads outward, unstoppable,
filling what it touches
with the weight of its fire,
its fragments embedded in all they meet.

but love sustains.
its burn holds,
like the steady heat of suns
spilling light across distances
it will never see.
what begins as force endures as rhythm,
etched into the patterns of a face,
or the warmth left in an empty room.

this is love,
to shatter and rebuild,
to store and release,
to remain in the universe it destroys,
and in the one it creates.

corinthian

love spoke, and the world unfolded,
a pulse impressed upon stone,
form drawn from stillness,
fire seeded in every chest.

love opened the hands to heal,
gave the tongue to shape what cannot be seen,
set wisdom to follow what does not fade,
each gift carried forward, meant for another.

a gong sounds, hollow,
a ringing without weight,
a hand striking only air.
work without love leaves no trace,
wisdom without love falls through the fingers,
sacrifice without love dissolves.

to heal is to move in love,
to teach is to let it speak,
to labor is to bear its weight,
to shape what changes by the measure of what endures.

prophecies rise, hopes crumble,
knowledge unravels in forgetting,
but love presses deeper,
woven in the seams of the hands,
laid down in the floor of what endures.
love forming, love filling,
the pulse beneath all things.

midnight

midnight holds stillness as the day yields to mystery.

*its poems dwell in silence and solitude, where rest
becomes a form of presence and song turns inward.*

*the cycle closes here, yet each ending gestures toward
beginning, for prayer will rise again with light.*

*the reader is invited to keep vigil in this hour, to let
silence prepare the heart for renewal.*

a psalm

o lord, who walks beside me always,
o lord, whose mercy knows no bounds,
come to me in my solitude,
in the depth of my foolish sorrow.

for the skies are cloaked in gray,
and my arm feels lost to the shadows;
my feet ache with burdens unseen,
and my thoughts are trapped within.

o lord of mercy, show mercy still,
for mercy is your endless gift.
o lord of love, pour love anew,
for love is the fullness of your being.

strengthen me, o lord, in my weakness;
lift my heart when it falters.
let me see you in the haze of my grief,
and feel you when the pain overwhelms.

in the stillness, may your presence rise,
let your voice resound.
though the skies grow dark, you are my light,
though i feel alone, you are my song.

o lord, teach my eyes to seek your face,
teach my hands to reach for you.
even when the clouds obscure the heavens,
let your mercy and love remain my guide.

stillness

even leaves dance.
i saw them just now,
responding
to a light breeze.

it is early in the spring,
and there are still desiccant reminders
of the fall,
twirling on their branches,
reveling in the sun,
reveling in this brisk morning light.

i saw the birds dance in the same way earlier.
they swung in a spherical pattern over the lake,
past the geese,
near the ducks,
twirling in endless rhythm.
some above me in the tree that loomed,
still without young leaves,
still thinking of the fall,
still dancing in the spring.

and yet,
i cannot dance.
not in spring,
or summer,
or fall,
or winter.

i cannot swing.
i cannot hear the music
that moves all of nature
except me.

stylite

i condemned myself to life,
set my back against a lecture hall.

shaped my torso into a column of stone.

i remain seated,
spilling sorrows from the ground.

pilgrims tilt their faces upward.
i remain below,
a stylite with no pillar,
a beggar folded into the floor.

in april

the hair along my arm
is bare against the cold
the trees along the path
bare against the grey.

branches extend into the damp air,
barren except to the closest eye,
where slow green sugars,
almost unseen.

rain coaxes silver from bark,
lingers on stone,
slips slow into skin.

i move through the wet ground,
no heavier than lint,
caught for a moment,
and then dissolved.

i weaken with the rain,
leaving behind all i carry.

the wet slips from bark to stone,
stone to skin,
skin to ground.

i sing once.
the rain sings once.
the earth sings once.

and the hidden psalm.

a comedy divine

must i go to florence,
or to a physicist
who might manipulate the material laws,
to walk with dante and the divine?
nothing could be more humourous
than a comedy
divine.
down into the depths we go.

you and i and the others.
to find humour
in life after death.

were there sadducees
and epicureans by our side,
this could all unfold
as faith.

winter archive

every winter, something vanishes.
last year, a finger and a heart
slipped beneath the snowbanks.
i still walk, compulsively,
too far from where i began,
too far to find what's missing.

the storm folds around me,
whispering its archive of limbs
and long-lost voices.
each step unearths fragments,
a pulse, a trace of warmth,
but never the whole.

this search for pieces,
buried or blown away,
is all i've learned of history.

quieter outside

it feels quieter outside when it snows,
the grey dome heavy with silence,
as if the world pauses to listen
to the fall of flakes.

here, the streets lie muted,
as if the pulse of business
has taken a holiday,
folding itself into rest.

elsewhere, there are lights,
the frantic weave of traffic,
the roar of lives colliding,
and the hero's pursuit
of lions and dragons.

the desert fathers knew these beasts,
their roaring hearts louder
in the silence of the desert
than in the cities they fled.

silence draws what is hidden to rise,
virtue sought in the taming
of unseen tigers,
their shadows leaping toward light.

snow falls like scripture,
its lines fleeting,
each flake writing
a new hush into the air.

in the stillness, the lions prowl,
their voices carried in the cold air,
yet the snow softens their steps,
each roar muffled, folded into quiet.

this silence, deeper than night,
wraps itself around me,
snuggles me into my moment,
its warmth stronger than the cold outside.

here, i rest, warm enough,
silent in the snow
each flake the bead on a string
of this day, as it slips away.

elsewhere, engines flare,
horns rise in discord,
and voices scatter,
chasing what cannot be caught.

here, snow smooths the edges,
a blanket laid across the noise.
its stillness carries no demands,
only the soft weight of peace.

the lions settle,
their movements fall to silence,
muffled in the falling snow.
more silent, like the falling snow.

winter falls like a second skin,
soft yet weighty,
pressing until silence
reveals its voice.

the universe holds me steady,
its arms drawn close,
its voice quiet and enduring,
each flake a fragile promise.

and i sit here, warm enough,
the snow falling outside,
the quiet folding around me
with the force of something eternal.

a walk in winter

snow falls, soft and endless,
the world folding itself into stillness.
each step draws us further,
the cold settling in, entire.

squirrels weave spirals around the trees,
their quickness a language
written into the frost,
a rhythm that never fades.

birds skim low, their wings
brushing light across the air.
their flight feels like a gesture,
brief and ungraspable.

the farmhouse leans into the earth,
its roof bending with the years.
its silence holds the snow,
the air around it still, listening.

there were sheep once,
their shadows part of the morning,
chickens scattering straw into the wind,
their feathers like bursts of light.

as children, we walked this path,
each turn alive with possibility.
the forest bent its branches toward us,
and the house drew life from the land.

this path held our parents' steps,
their voices woven into the forest.
they are here still,
their rhythm folded into the trees.

the snow drifts in silver strands,

the current pulling it sideways.
it rushes at our faces,
its sharpness pushing us inward.

our hoods rise against the cold,
our voices falling back into silence.
each step folds into the frost,
the world softening as we move.

we walk crookedly now,
slower, more deliberate.
time leans into our movements,
its weight steady, familiar.

the river curves ahead,
its edges held by the forest.
beneath the ice, water turns slowly,
its surface rippled where snow has melted.

the earth shifts beneath us,
each step catching on the edge of softness.
the ground feels thin,
its frailty carried in the sound of our feet.

fallen trunks stretch like ruins,
their forms rigid as ancient columns.
we think of cappadocia and cyprus,
the way stone remembers its shaping.

their hollows hold the draft,
a low voice moving through the forest.
the trees rise taller each year,
their roots gripping what we lose.

memory moves with us,
the paths we ran as children,
the times we let the world pull us forward,
the weight of joy before we knew its cost.

the breeze presses against us,
its voice alive, carving shapes
into the snow. we feel its presence
pushing us, then moving ahead.

squirrels scatter behind us,
their laughter curling into the branches.
their spirals never break,
a rhythm eternal, circling the forest.

the farmhouse disappears into shadow,
its story held beneath the snow.
what lingers is its quiet weight,
its presence folded into memory.

the snow falls like scripture,
each flake a fleeting verse.
we walk within its brief gospel,
our steps dissolving beneath us.

the snow thickens as we move,
its weight brushing at our boots.
it asks for stillness,
each step slower, the air clearer.

we walk together, our silence
woven into the rhythm of the forest.
the trees seem to exhale,
their presence endless.

the snow softens and stills.
the forest stands unbroken,
its hours scored in frost.

somewhere in between

january hush settles
across wooden fences,
a soft presence
glimpsed in frosted panes,
behind drawn curtains

mallalieu wonders
where truth resides,
its shape never pinned down
like a bird in flight.
empedocles whispers
of love and strife.

i listen to homilies astray in a podcast.
words drifting in low light,
questions folding
into the quiet edges
of my thoughts.

somewhere in between
the hush of dusk
and the tune of tomorrow,
truth flickers
against cold glass,
or the faint glow
we sense through walls.

i linger here,
turning each line of poetry
like an ember in hand.
naming it,
i bring it closer,
or simply trace
its echo in the stillness.

ages dark

there were dark periods,
times when the muses slept,
and the hands that shaped history moved in silence.
byzantium stands as it was.
it remains as we are.
its echoes lingering in the stones we walk upon,
its shadows traced in the light of our creations.

the sources we draw from,
the wisdom that fills our books of leadership,
the forms of the temples where we kneel,
all find their beginnings there.
we are as byzantine as the byzantines,
who called themselves romans,
and sometimes greeks.

the past is never distant,
its roots entwined with ours,
its monuments crumbled into whispers,
yet still they guide our hands.

in narrow rooms

beneath these low ceilings,
voices stacking themselves
against the air,
layered as if they had weight.

hooks line the parapets,
a procession of coats,
their folds heavy with dust
or memory.
a hand might touch one,
and the cloth would lift,
opening into wings.

what lingers:
the faint trace of laughter,
sharp and brittle,
or the scrape of iron,
something heavy dragged
slowly across stone.

at etna

bronze sandals rest at the edge,
leather frayed where the straps have loosened.
the slope propels ash in waves,
soft and rising,
each grain scattering before it settles.

feet leave prints that disappear,
each step lighter,
less body, more motion.
there is no pause,
only the curve of a leap,
a gesture bound to the air,
to the glow that reaches upward.

no sound carries here
but the faint exhale of ash
folding into itself.
bronze cools beneath the dust,
its curve gleaming faintly.
a note held long past silence.

volcano

were i to stand by this volcano
and summon its fires,
call them by their ancient names,
drawn in ash and smoke,
would you quit this sadness,
watching me as if i were moses
in the movie,
hair turned white by god?

except it would be different.
tablets left unshaped,
commandments unspoken,
only the slow collapse of my form,
skin lifting like paper from bone.

i would speak until my throat burned,
until every syllable rose
and broke against the air,
a sacrifice given
for the chance you might see me,
briefly,
whole in my undoing.

the gods would pass,
untouched by fire.
the sky would stay empty
while i,
stripped to story,
ask only
that you look.

and the sadness
would return.

daemon

i sway,
bowing at the knee,
bending at the back.
i flow where the wind may blow.
i stay.

water moves.
i yield,
a surface parted,
a current folding over stone.
i flow where the river goes.
i stay.

fire climbs.
i lift my hands,
palms open to the heat,
skin thinned by flame.
i flow where the fire goes.
i stay.

earth holds.
i press my body down,
shoulder to soil,
life into dust.
i flow where the earth is still.
i stay.

what moves returns.
what yields endures.
i move as water moves,
as wind, as fire, as stone.
i flow where the wind may blow.
i stay.

time may bend

i came to you when there was good weather.
even when it rained, we stood in the light.
haircuts of youth, the tightness of skin,
laughter bent through crowded rooms,
the air warm with the press of bodies.

we spoke in voices bright as sunlit glass,
the road unfurled in silver streams,
its bends shimmering like water catching light,
boundless, untouched by shadow,
stretching through the bend of time.

now it is autumn, now winter.
the days contract, air sharpens.
where are you, and where am i,
as roots withdrawn into earth,
as a cellar that maintains silence.

the seasons advance without pause,
i remain among the falling branches,
listening for what was once near,
hearing only the scrape of silence,
the outline of what remains.

and finding only traces folded
into the hollow of my palm,
soft as sweetness remembered,
like the taste of memory,
lingering, though the glow slips to shadows.

in three steps

at the edge of the clearing,
roots clutch fractured ground,
weeds rise sharp into air,
pulling the unseen earth close.
the road bristles with shadows,
their edges pressed inward by stillness.

hands stretch into the dim,
the weight of faith trembling at their ends.
rain gathers in soft clay,
pooling beneath the ribs,
its pull steady, urging forward.

a thread of light spills ahead,
its rhythm loosening the still air into paths.
each step pulls at a knot buried deep,
its strands tightening before they fall away.
what the feet uncover, the body follows,
each movement carving space
where none was clear before.

beneath the surface, roots pull gently,
a whisper, almost pleading,
but the light threads onward,
its rhythm unbroken,
its quiet pulse an answer
only motion can reveal.

the city sways with restless rhythms,
its pulse carried by engines and footsteps.
steel arches bend under the weight of hours,
pavement gleams with the shimmer of rain.
faces pass in fleeting shapes,
their outlines sensed but never held.

freedom gathers in quiet places.
light pooling in cracks of stone,
lifting what clings too tightly.
its touch falls softly,
its absence sharper than glass
scattered beneath hurried steps.

footsteps scatter across shallow puddles,
each ripple pulling the street into motion.
most quicken their pace
as voices, and screens, and blinking lights.
freedom swells in their veins,
before spilling away,
like water slipping from cupped hands.

one among us slows.
their steps falter;
the road bends backward,
the quiet pulls closer,
its weight presses steady,
like a hand resting against the chest.
what lingers is thick in the air,
a presence woven into the stillness.
they listen,
alive with waiting.

evening moves across the street,
velvet-soft against the edges of thought.
the air gathers itself,
dense with stillness,
holding all that daylight spilled.

to return gathers what was offered,
faith settling into spaces carved by motion.
the source moves steadily beneath shifting ground,
its presence an anchor,
its gift unwavering.

faith rises with each step,
a rhythm that steadies the body
it turns the road into prayer,
the day into its own psalter.

hands that stretched toward the dim
now hold the fullness of return,
grateful for the quiet light
that led them home.

the road stretches forward,
its line steady beneath the settling sky.
each step leaves a trail of stillness
filling itself with light.

against the stillness
beneath the iron bridge the creek drags dark,
a thread drawn tight across the earth.
squirrels leap branch to branch,
tails snapping like sparks in a gale.

each leap holds the cold at bay,
each twist defies the drift toward silence.
their paws quicken against bark,
alive in every flicker,
alive in every pulse.

the earth leans toward winter,
yet they scurry against its pull,
as if frost could be outrun,
as if night might never close.

soon the day will thin,
but for now they race through the branches,
stirring heat through the trees,
wild in their rhythm.

the quiet will come,
hollows will gather their rest,
but not yet,
not yet.

the streets in january

between snows, after snow, before the next.
sidewalks salted heavy,
ploughs carving paths without plan.
we squint under a sun too sharp,
search for coats thick as armor,
pockets crammed with mittens, damp gloves.

near the school, children spill into the snow,
wrapped in purple plastic, bright against the drift.
some lie still, angels frozen mid-chorus.
others hurl snowballs skyward,
aiming for their god,
or scream into the cold for reasons unknown.

these are old days and new memories,
or old memories dressed in today's snow.
i walk in circles,
lost yet tethered to time.
green roofs, brown roofs,
shingles crusted white.
cars vanish beneath stiff blankets of white.
trees stand bare, waiting,
their nests hollow as promises.

my steps grow louder,
children's voices fade.
this is the story of my life:
running from where i am
to arrive where i began.

i cannot wish it otherwise.
this is the best of all worlds.
this is the best of all things.
this is the best of all worlds, she whispered.
this is the best of things, i murmured back.

i imagine the world watching me
walk through perpendicular streets.
the same faces pass, and i pass them too.
until tomorrow,
or some other day.

destruction belongs to unity

destruction belongs to unity,
said anaxagoras somewhere outside lampascus,
as he watched slaves and animals labor in the olive mill.

green fruit, unripe but plucked in mid-november,
before frost stiffened its flesh,
was fed to the grinding stone,
its skin torn open,
its pulp crushed, releasing its hidden fire.

the fruit bled its light,
a stream that softened the grind of ancient wheels,
that lit winter rooms,
that slicked the palms of gods and lovers alike.
it surrendered its stone heart,
splintered and scattered,
to heat the hearths of the living
and kindle the beginnings of fire.

anaxagoras, or perhaps pythagoras,
might have paused to see the greater cycle:
the olive, born from the earth's quiet violence,
from roots wrestling the soil,
from sun's fire and the long fall of rain,
now giving itself whole,
oil, warmth, ash,
to the endless work of the world.

the stone turns, steady and unyielding,
while love and disdain move through the millstones too,
pressing themselves into the substance of what remains.
the olive's brief, heroic life,
from spring's fragile bud
to the thick, golden liquid
that feeds, that burns, that sustains,
becoming a testament of surrender and transformation.

destruction, whispered anaxagoras,
is no end but a beginning:
to break is to bind,
to crush is to release.
unity lives in the giving,
in the stone's press and the fruit's bending.

and so the olive becomes a teacher,
its journey, inimitable,
a mirror to all things brief and essential,
the hands that pick and press,
the fire that feeds and consumes,
the world turning slowly
under the millstone's endless spin.

those words

those words
were jagged, glass-bitten, bitter with bile,
cutting like sea-glass, rounded to deceive,
cruel in how they slid beneath the skin.

and yet,
they carried the faint scent of cheap roses,
petals fading before water reached them,
fragrance plastic, designed to mislead.

they lingered exquisitely,
a whisper too sweet to distrust,
coiling in air,
silken on the tongue,
barbs hidden beneath the gloss.

each syllable deliberate,
a chisel against stone,
not to form beauty,
but to strip raw the core.

these words left no bruises,
only echoes, endless,
churning in the chest,
a melody off-key, impossible to ignore.

was it intent, or artistry,
that made them wound so beautifully.
the speaker, bow drawn across taut strings,
carved anguish into sound.
even silence that followed
was deliberate,
a pause for venom to sink.

what can one do
when words bloom like weeds,
taking root in the soul,
hardening the soft earth of memory
into stone.

beneath the roses,
a garden tangled with wildflowers and nettles,
beauty sharp, undeniable.
still,
there was craftsmanship,
exquisite pain,
precision in the strike.

eternity traces in the lines on a pew

a hand moves along carved wood,
lines curling deep into years.
the grain carries each touch,
its arcs remembering.

voices rise, layered and slow,
binding human rhythm to wood.
sound threads every corner,
its cadence unbroken.

incense drifts through the air,
folding into hidden places,
settling in the carved lines,
an offering absorbed.

icons gleam faintly in gold,
woven into the same rhythm.
their stillness belongs to the chant,
part of its weaving.

the hand moves again,
joining the wood's motion.
arcs bend forward,
continuous, whole.

this is the hymn:
carved into wood,
lifted in song,
carried by incense.

between sand and moon

the beach is endless, vast and high,
a mountain of sand beneath the sky,
pulverized stone, the broken shells,
a song of tides the ocean tells.

the waters ebb in turquoise light,
recede in charcoal, day to night.
they touch the shore, inhale and flow,
chanting a hymn, unhurried, slow.

umbrellas scatter, shadows lean,
the sun melts dreams into the scene.
sweat beads gather, hopes unwind,
a rhythm lost, a threadless bind.

the beach strums a quiet tune,
waves loosening lines of heat from skin.
the moon glitters in broken pieces on the tide,
each shard carried shoreward, then drawn away,
a rhythm stitched between sand and sky.

a still place

the lake stays silent.
light strikes
the surface.
a heron folds inward,
wings close,
body hidden.

the reeds bend as you near,
their movement slight.
your reflection appears,
familiar, broken by ripples,
a shape passing
just beneath.

drifting air crosses the water.
its sound a low rustle,
its touch along the shore.
rings widen,
then vanish.

the surface holds.
shadow and self blur.
only the lake remains.

slip through transcendence

lasers move on the ceiling,
red, blue, green,
slipping through the curtain's edge,
quiet stitches in the dark.
fifteen hundred points of light scatter,
shifting patterns down the halls,
finding me as sleep begins.

the glow dances with imagination through the house,
brushing the windows,
resting its colors on frostbitten grass.
tonight, for the first time in weeks,
i watched them in the dining room,
a place i pass but rarely pause.
the colors gathered on the table,
a quiet tide curling over corners,
slipping into the empty chairs.

outside, snow drifted in steady falls,
flakes catching the lasers' light,
flashing, spinning, then vanishing,
a scatter of sparks drawn upward by force.
light and snow wove together,
falling, rising,
a fleeting song the cold could not abate.

what a jocund day, i thought,
though it was midnight,
and the darkness pressed against the windows.
the house creaked under my steps,
but the light moved on,
like a fragile rhythm,
until the words began to form,
and i drifted into their glow.

where is home

when the robin near the front stoop
stops picking through the yellow grass
which has survived the winter
and flaps its wings abruptly,
lifting itself onto your forehead,
gripping your skin with its tiny talons
and lifts you both swiftly into the sky.

the lake water appears grey
as the scales of dragons
rippling with rage.

the white flecks are ice and glass.

the light breaks,
and you break in two,
too tall to fly and too light to sink.

until it is time to say goodnight.

nunc dimittis

let me go, my lord.
i have seen your glory.
i have held the edge of dawn
before the sun was free.

the years have gathered,
heavy as smoke in the temple air,
folding silence into silence,
turning with the stars.

i have touched the place of pain,
set my hands to the wound
where time leaks into eternity,
where suffering holds steady
beneath the bones of the world.

yet now my eyes are full,
brimmed with the flame you set in the dark,
a fire to split the night,
a blade to lift the veil.

let me go, my lord.
my hands are emptied of longing.
my lips have opened the threshold.
i step into stillness,
where time bends,
where light is not lost.

Author Bio Note:

Theodore Michael Christou is Professor of Education at Queen's University. He has held faculty and administrative positions at Ontario Tech University and the University of New Brunswick. Theodore has published broadly in the areas of educational history and curriculum studies but remains devoted to a life in and with poetry. A life-long educator, Dr. Christou is a member of the Ontario College of Teachers and the College of Early Childhood Educators. Theodore has lectured and taught internationally in the fields of history education, philosophy of education, curriculum theory, and social impact. He lives in Kingston, Ontario, with his wife Glenda and their wonderful dog, Bernie.

Table of Contents

Introduction – *p. ix*

– orthros – *p. 1*
– in the breath of the tree – *p. 2*
– a world arranged with grace – *p. 4*
– humid light – *p. 5*
– echoes of fragility – *p. 6*
– the river – *p. 7*
– i come to home – *p. 8*
– vasileion – *p. 9*
– ways of walking – *p. 10*
– the way a river changes – *p. 12*
– boundless – *p. 14*
– mercy in the frost – *p. 16*
– fresh as snow – *p. 17*
– it is a new day – *p. 19*
– some mornings – *p. 20*
– threads of flight – *p. 21*
– how we build the light – *p. 23*
– the light between us – *p. 24*
– winter love – *p. 25*
– rest day – *p. 26*
– seven suns – *p. 27*
– thick with light – *p. 29*
– as water moves – *p. 31*
– first hour – *p. 33*
– mercy in the morning – *p. 34*
– reasons i fold my clothes in silence – *p. 35*
– inventory of threadbare things – *p. 36*
– day to day – *p. 37*
– storm door soprano – *p. 40*
– the same stone – *p. 41*
– intercostal – *p. 42*
– askizometha – *p. 43*
– deal with the universe – *p. 46*
– clinamen – *p. 47*
– third hour – *p. 49*

– parvati and the gull – *p. 50*
– let me be loved – *p. 52*
– fearsome love – *p. 53*
– gregory's flame – *p. 54*
– the heraclitean god – *p. 55*
– empedoclean – *p. 56*
– see the moon – *p. 58*
– petrarch's garden – *p. 59*
– between the apocalypses – *p. 61*
– we are those summer leaves – *p. 62*
– open field – *p. 63*
– salt thick on the tongue – *p. 64*
– lost beyond the path – *p. 65*
– the weight – *p. 66*
– i die daily – *p. 67*
– oblate poet – *p. 69*
– down to the ice – *p. 70*
– palpitation – *p. 72*
– endoscope – *p. 73*
– tidewater – *p. 74*
– altar of frost – *p. 75*
– the thud – *p. 78*
– this little bird – *p. 82*
– the sway – *p. 83*
– permanency and the snow – *p. 84*
– cataclysm – *p. 85*
– the ant – *p. 86*
– anche io – *p. 87*
– corpus manifesto – *p. 88*
– thirty pieces – *p. 89*
– feel of blood – *p. 90*
– in the palaces – *p. 91*
– when light came – *p. 92*
– the river we remember swirls – *p. 93*
– he ran – *p. 95*
– adamantine – *p. 96*
– skotos – *p. 97*

– still it flows – *p. 99*
– the sea vast – *p. 100*
– the sadducee's shrug – *p. 101*
– the vines – *p. 102*
– pretty lies – *p. 103*
– the last – *p. 104*
– once again and again – *p. 105*
– the one who stays – *p. 110*
– the horizon gives way – *p. 111*
– wax and parchment – *p. 112*
– unmoving – *p. 113*
– the relic – *p. 114*
– there are depths of solitude – *p. 115*
– when light waits – *p. 116*
– echo of heat – *p. 117*
– tulips in bloom – *p. 118*
– o grow too thick – *p. 119*
– texture of light – *p. 120*
– shape – *p. 122*
– love too vast for silence – *p. 123*
– inheritance – *p. 124*
– this is how we go – *p. 126*
– rooted stillness – *p. 127*
– crossing – *p. 128*
– days of creation – *p. 129*
– while the world unravels – *p. 131*
– sycamore – *p. 133*
– one cold day – *p. 137*
– i have walked this city – *p. 144*
– florence again – *p. 146*
– i sang her song – *p. 147*
– for inspiration – *p. 148*
– cyprian – *p. 149*
– alas for – *p. 150*
– do not trust me – *p. 151*
– we are drawn toward knowledge – *p. 152*
– cosmopolitan – *p. 153*
– the halls are quiet – *p. 154*
– the train – *p. 156*

– losing the measure of myself – *p. 157*
– rolling hills – *p. 158*
– see and snow – *p. 160*
– name my moon – *p. 162*
– the wheel – *p. 163*
– morning's balance – *p. 164*
– squared light – *p. 165*
– corinthian – *p. 166*
– a psalm – *p. 170*
– stillness – *p. 171*
– stylite – *p. 172*
– in april – *p. 173*
– a comedy divine – *p. 174*
– winter archive – *p. 175*
– quieter outside   – *p. 176*
– a walk in winter – *p. 178*
– somewhere in between – *p. 181*
– ages dark – *p. 182*
– in narrow rooms – *p. 183*
– at etna – *p. 184*
– volcano – *p. 185*
– daemon – *p. 186*
– time may bend – *p. 187*
– in three steps – *p. 188*
– the streets in january – *p. 191*
– destruction belongs to unity – *p. 193*
– those words – *p. 195*
– eternity traces in the lines on a pew – *p. 197*
– between sand and moon – *p. 198*
– a still place – *p. 199*
– slip through transcendence – *p. 200*
– where is home – *p. 201*
– nunc dimittis – *p. 202*

Author Bio Note – *p. 205*